TAX PLANNING FOR INVESTORS

A Guide to Securities Investment and Tax Shelters

TAX PLANNING FOR INVESTORS

A Guide to Securities Investment and Tax Shelters

Jack Crestol, CPA, JD, LLM

COOPERS & LYBRAND

and

Herman M. Schneider, CPA, JD, LLM

COOPERS & LYBRAND

DOW JONES BOOKS
PRINCETON, NEW JERSEY

This publication is designed to provide accurate and authoritative information in regard to the subject matter covered. It is sold with the understanding that the publisher is not engaged in rendering legal, accounting, or other professional service. If legal advice or other expert assistance is required, the services of a competent professional person should be sought.

From a Declaration of Principles jointly adopted by a Committee of the American Bar Association and a Committee of Publishers.

Published by Dow Jones Books
P.O. Box 300, Princeton, NJ 08540

Copyright 1978 by Dow Jones & Company, Inc.

Printed and bound in the United States of America
10 9 8 7 6

Library of Congress Cataloging in Publication Data

Crestol, Jack.
  Tax planning for investors.

  Includes index.
  1. Investments—Taxation—United States.
2. Taxation of bonds, securities, etc.—United States.
3. Capital gains tax—United States. 4. Tax shelters—
Law and legislation—United States. I. Schneider,
Herman M., joint author. II. Title.
KE6415.C73 1979   343'.73'052   79-10505

ISBN 0-87128-574-6

TABLE OF CONTENTS

II. PRINCIPLES OF TAXATION OF SECURITIES TRANSACTIONS

PREFACE

The investor's primary objective in investing in securities is to make a profit: buy low, sell high. Unfortunately, however, getting the *most* profit from a year's security transactions is not a simple matter of buying low and selling high, because the tax laws determine how much of the profit can be kept.

The informed investor measures his economic gain or yield in terms of after-tax dollars or the amount of additional cash available after considering all expenses including income taxes. It should be emphasized, however, that although the informed investor should be highly conscious of tax factors, he will rarely allow these tax factors to affect an economic decision. A short-term gain taxed at ordinary rates is still superior to a long-term capital loss, no matter how heavily the gain is taxed. Nevertheless, in many instances taxes can be minimized with little or no economic effect.

To aid investors in their understanding of how security transactions and other types of investments are taxed and the kind of planning measures necessary to maximize the after-tax gain, this book was first issued in 1966 and revised in 1967 and 1970. It has again been revised to reflect new developments, including the Tax Reform Act of 1976 (1976 TRA) and the Revenue Act of 1978 (1978 RA), and now provides in Part I a list of tax saving opportunities and in Part II a summary of the tax rules an investor needs to know to plan effectively. This book is not intended to show investors how to realize economic gains in securities transactions, but rather how to obtain the best tax advantages in recognizing gains or losses. To this end, tax savings opportunities are discussed in the form of objectives, such as postponing tax recognition of gain, converting short-term gains into long-term gains, etc. For example, the investor may be able to create a long-term gain and an approximately equivalent short-term loss in the same or different years by acquiring a commodity straddle (the purchase and short sale of the same commodity future calling for delivery in different months), while at the same time achieving his intended economic objectives.

The provisions of the Revenue Act of 1978 will affect all investors, but will have an extra beneficial effect on high-tax bracket individuals who benefit from the 50 percent maximum tax on personal service income. The principal changes affecting investors are (i) decreased tax rates and an increase in personal exemptions to $1,000, (ii) an increase in the capital gains deduction from 50 percent to 60 percent, (iii) repeal of the 25 percent alternative tax on long-term capital gains, (iv) the capital gains deduction will no longer affect the maximum tax on personal service income, (v) in lieu of a 15 percent minimum tax on capital gains deductions, there will be a separate alternative tax which will not apply to most investors, (vi) carryover basis at death rules are deferred, and (vii) additional restrictions are placed in the case of tax shelters. These and other changes will be discussed in detail in the text.

This book is concerned primarily with the Federal tax liabilities of an individual filing his income tax return on a cash basis. Although many of the ideas presented and the discussion of the relevant income tax provisions may also apply (with or without some modification) to non-resident aliens, traders, dealers, partnerships, trusts, estates and corporations, the text does not consider such possible application. However, there are separate chapters summarizing the tax effects for non-resident alien investors, corporations, trusts, estates and other types of investors. In addition, the discussion is confined primarily to transactions in securities of publicly owned corporations, and although many of these provisions apply also to closely-held corporations, it does not consider the special tax provisions relating to closely-held or related corporations. In all the examples, it is assumed that the investor files his tax return on the calendar year basis. Furthermore, for the sake of simplicity, a capital gains tax of 25 percent is used, although for most investors the effective tax rate will be lower. In addition, a more than one-year holding period for long-term capital gains will be used in the text although there were transitional rules for pre-1978 taxable years. Unless otherwise indicated, all examples are applicable under the Revenue Act of 1978.

For practical reasons, State and local tax liabilities are not considered herein. Such liabilities are usually small in relation to Federal tax liabilities and are frequently computed on comparable bases. The investor is warned, however, that situations may arise where State or local tax liabilities may be large enough to influence an investor's tax planning. Each investor should acquaint himself with the nature and magnitude of such taxes as they apply to him.

For the convenience of the reader, the discussion of tax savings opportunities is cross-referenced to the discussion of tax principles. Official authorities are referred to in footnotes and indexed in the appendix, and both a detailed word index of subject matters and a detailed table of contents are provided. Many readers will prefer first to scan the tax savings opportunities for interesting suggestions and then to read the sections of Part II that apply.

The authors wish to acknowledge their appreciation of the invaluable assistance of their associates in the offices of Coopers & Lybrand. In particular, Norman E. Auerbach, CPA, James B. Fish, Jr., CPA, Joseph M. Lobel, Anthony P. Rua, CPA, and Warren G. Wintrub, CPA, assisted in preparation of the earlier editions and/or this revision.

Jack Crestol
Herman M. Schneider

New York, N.Y.

TAX SAVINGS OPPORTUNITIES

INTRODUCTION

The ideas discussed in this section are intended to present the investor with alternative legitimate methods of casting a transaction so that the investor can either reduce his tax liability or defer the tax to another year. Many of these ideas have been sanctioned by court decisions or by Treasury regulations or rulings. However, the investor should be aware that the Treasury may attack tax savings transactions on various grounds, sometimes despite court approval of the transaction.

The trading in Listed options on several exchanges has recently become a very popular form of investment. However, for many sophisticated investors, Unlisted options are still being utilized. Accordingly, portions of this section dealing with options will cover all options, but certain sections will be applicable to only Unlisted options. Under such circumstances, such limitations will be clearly indicated.

The illustrations generally do not take into consideration the transaction costs, i.e., commissions, applicable transfer taxes and so forth. Accordingly, such costs must be considered in the overall economics of the transaction.

It is appropriate at this point to reemphasize the importance of the economics of a transaction aside from the tax considerations. The courts and the Internal Revenue Service more and more have been looking into the pre-tax economics of the transaction. The investor

1

cannot have recognized for tax purposes a transaction he enters into solely for tax reasons with no expectations of ever realizing a profit on the transaction.[1] However, the existence of economic profit potential should be sufficient. Notwithstanding, the Internal Revenue Service has recently ruled that the short-term capital loss generated in a commodity straddle transaction results in no real economic loss and is not deductible.[2] This position of the government fails to recognize the total economic and profit potential of commodity straddle transactions, but is indicative of the emphasis that is being placed on "pre-tax economics". Accordingly, the economic and profit potential of the tax saving opportunities discussed below must be considered.

POSTPONE TAX RECOGNITION OF GAIN OR LOSS

The transactions discussed below will postpone the recognition of the gain or loss, but will not change the character of the gain or loss when recognized for tax purposes. Several of the ideas have general application, while others are limited to specific types of investments.

"Short Against the Box" An investor can sell a security but defer the recognition of gain until the next year by selling short an equal number of shares and covering the short sale in the following year with the shares originally held. This is commonly known as "selling short against the box." Ordinarily, the long-term or short-term nature of the gain will be determined at the time of the short sale and therefore will not be affected by the deferral. However, in the case of securities held for more than six months, care should be taken to ensure that long-term capital gain treatment will result under the post-1976 transitional rules for long-term capital gains. (See page 85). The amount of tax on the gain will depend on the taxpayer's other income, other tax preference items, and the tax rates in effect in the year in which the gain is recognized. Deferral of the gain, therefore, may result in a higher or lower effective tax rate on the gain, and should be taken into account in determining whether or not to go short against the box. A deferral of gain may be particularly effective where an investor has a change in economic status, e.g., retirement from his position. By delaying long-term

---

[1] Goldstein, 364 F2d 734 (CA-2, 1966)   [2] Rev. Rul. 77-185, I.R.B. 1977-21,7

capital gains until after retirement, there may not only be a drop in overall income, but the tax preferences created by the long-term gains may no longer affect the maximum tax on personal service income.

> *Example:* An investor may wish to protect his profit in stock acquired on November 1, 1977 for $20 per share, and which is selling on December 1, 1978 for $50. Instead of recognizing a $30 per share long-term capital gain in 1978, the investor could sell short the stock at $50 and defer the closing of such sale until January of 1979, at which time the long-term gain of $30 per share (less transfer fees and taxes) will be recognized. If the stock was acquired on December 15, 1977, so that the holding period of the stock was not more than one year at the time of the short sale, the gain recognized upon the closing of the short sale would be a short-term capital gain. (See discussion of short sales, pages 83 to 91.)

The short sale may also be used to sell a depreciated security but defer the recognition of the loss until the next year. Ordinarily it is more advantageous to deduct the loss in the current year. However, under certain circumstances, it may be more beneficial taxwise to postpone recognizing the loss. The following are some examples where the losses should be postponed.

> *Example (a):* *Excess deductions:* T's deductions exceed his income, including $3,000 of capital gains, by $5,000. On December 1, T wants to sell a stock and realize a capital loss of $2,000. There would be no tax benefit if the capital loss is recognized in the current year because there is no taxable income and the excess deductions cannot be carried to another year. (See page 47.) A short sale of the stock will enable T to apply the capital loss against his income in the year the sale is closed.

> *Example (b):* *Long-term loss and short-term gain:* In 1977, T has realized $10,000 of short-term gains and $10,000 of long-term losses. He expects to realize short-term gains and long-term gains in 1978. T has suffered a $6,000 loss on a stock acquired late in 1977 and wants to sell it before there is a further drop in its value. By selling the stock short and closing it early in 1978, T can offset his 1977

3

long-term losses against his short-term gains and offset the postponed $6,000 short-term loss against his 1978 short-term gains. If he recognized the loss in 1977, the loss would be applied against his 1977 short-term gains. However, only $4,000 of the $10,000 long-term loss could be offset against the remaining 1977 short-term gains, $4,000 of the loss would be applied against $2,000 of his 1977 ordinary income (see page 62) and $2,000 of the long-term loss would be offset against 1978 long-term gains. T would obtain an additional $2,000 deduction in 1977, but at the expense of having $6,000 more of short-term gains in 1978 and only a $2,000 reduction in long-term gains.

Example (c): *Transitional rule:* A long-term capital loss can be converted into a short-term capital loss under the transitional rule. To illustrate, T acquired a stock on February 1, 1977 for $10,000. On December 15, 1977 the stock is selling at $6,000 and T wishes to sell the stock because he expects the price to go down even further. A sale in 1977 would result in a $4,000 long-term loss which could be offset against long-term gains, or if no gains, against $2,000 of ordinary income. By selling the stock short, T can limit his economic loss and by covering the short sale before February 2, 1978, the long-term loss is changed into a short-term loss under the one-year holding period rule in effect for 1978. The short-term loss can now be offset against short-term gains in 1978, or if there are no gains, against $3,000 of ordinary income on a dollar to dollar basis and the remaining $1,000 short-term loss carried into 1979.

Example (d): *Income averaging:* As a result of the income averaging rules (see page 142), T can pay a low tax on his capital gains in 1977. T expects short-term gains in 1978 and expects to pay a much larger tax on his 1978 gains. T has incurred a $5,000 loss on a security and wants to sell it before there is a further decline. By selling short in 1977 and closing in 1978, T can obtain a greater tax benefit from the loss.

Example (e): *Maximum tax on personal service income:* T's annual salary is $100,000. His tax preference items ordinarily are less than $10,000, but in 1978 he expects to exercise qualified stock options which will increase his total tax preference items by $25,000. (See page 140.) He has an unrealized loss on a stock of $10,000 which he can apply against his capital gains in 1977 or 1978. By selling short in 1977 and covering in 1978, T may increase the amount of wages that will be subject to a maximum tax of 50 percent rather than 70 percent. By deferring the loss, T will have a greater tax for 1977, but there will be a substantial decrease in tax for the two-year period.

Under certain circumstances, the broker may release to the investor a substantial portion of the funds arising from the short sale or allow the purchase of other securities with the purchasing power created because of such short sale. Interest will ordinarily be charged on the short sale. The investor should determine the position of his broker in this situation before making the short sale. It may be possible to keep both positions open for a long period of time, have the use of the funds or additional purchasing power during this period, and still avoid recognition of gain.

Due to the deferral of the new basis carryover provision, it is possible during the interim period to avoid tax on the unrecognized gain if the investor died before the short-sale was closed. Should the investor die after the interim period, a determination would have to be made whether closing the short-sale before or after death would result in a savings of overall taxes.

Acquisition of a Put

The investor can defer the recognition of any gain on his stock and still minimize the possible reduction in the amount of his gain by acquiring an option to sell the stock (a "Put"). The advantage of this method as compared to the use of a short sale, as discussed above, is that in the event the stock continues to rise, the investor obtains the benefit of such rise. However, the cost of acquiring this insurance against decline is normally in the area of 10 to 15 percent of the value of the underlying security. This varies in accordance with the period of time that the option will run, the volatility of the stock, and supply and demand for the Put. A tax disadvantage under either method is that if the underlying security is held less than one year at the time of the short sale or acquisition of the Put, any gain on subsequent sale will generally be treated as short-term, since the holding period of the stock will not begin until the short sale is covered or the Put is exercised, expires or is disposed of. (See discussion of short sales on page 86.)

It is not expected that Listed Puts will have a duration of more than nine months and accordingly, long-term capital gain potential on the sale of Listed Puts will not be available. However, Unlisted Puts for more than one year will be available and can be utilized to accord the investor potential long-term capital gain treatment upon ultimate sale.

Example: Assume that an investor owned stock acquired July 1, 1978 at $20 per share, and he purchased on December 1, 1978 a one year, 10 day Unlisted Put at $50 for the equivalent of $5 per share. The investor then has the right to "put" or sell the stock to the writer of the option at any time during the period for $50 per share, regardless of the then selling price of the stock. If the market value of the stock rises, for example, to $75 per share and the investor wishes to close out the transaction, he can sell the stock in the open market, recognizing a $55 per share, short-term capital gain (the stock was held for less than one year at the time the Put was acquired). He would try to sell the Put prior to the end of the one year period, realizing a short-term loss of approximately $5 per share, in lieu of merely letting the Put expire, in which case the loss would be long-term.

If the investor had sold short the stock at $50 per share in lieu of acquiring the Put, he would have limited his gain to $30 per share. Thus, for a cost of approximately $5 per share, the Put insures a minimum gain and allows potentially substantial gain possibilities for the one year period in the event of a rise in the stock market.

If the market value of the stock should fall, for example, to $30 per share by December 2, 1979 (Put held for more than one year), he would sell the Put for the equivalent price of approximately $20 per share ($50 option price less market value of stock of $30) and, therefore, recognize long-term gain of approximately $15 per share ($20 per share proceeds less $5 per share cost of the Put). The stock would then be sold for $30, resulting in a capital gain of $10 per share which is given *short-term* treatment even though the stock was held for more than one year. This occurs with respect to the gain because at the time of the acquisition of the Put, such shares were held for less than one year, thus bringing in effect the short sale rules. If the stock were instead sold for $15 per share, a *loss* of $5 per share would be treated as *long-term*, since the short sale rules would not be applicable. See page 59 for discussion of transitional rules concerning holding period for long-term gains in 1976, 1977 and 1978.

A discussion of the seller's option is to be found on page 19. Selling via this route will enable the seller to take advantage of the current market price and still defer recognition of gain and add up to 60 days to his holding period. Thus, a seller who has held a security for from ten months to one year can convert a short-term gain into a long-term gain without further exposure to market risk.

Deferred Delivery Under New York Stock Exchange Rule 64(3) (Seller's Option)

A cash-basis investor selling stock toward the end of his taxable year may control which year the gain is to be recognized. When stock is sold in the "regular way," as is the case in most instances, the settlement day will be the fifth business day following the trade date. A loss will be recognized in the year in which the trade date falls, but a profit is not taxable until the subsequent year in which the settlement date falls. The cash-basis investor may cause the gain to be recognized in the year of the trade by making the sale "for cash." (See page 19 dealing with deferred delivery under N.Y. Stock Exchange Rule 64(3) for possible postponement of gain for up to 60 days.) For year end sales in 1976 and 1977 the transitional holding period rules must be taken into account or a long-term gain in the earlier year will be converted into a short-term gain if the sale is made in the subsequent year without meeting the longer holding period requirements for the year of sale. On the other hand, a long-term loss can be changed into a short-term loss by delaying the sale until the next year. (See page 59).

Year-End Sales

When Listed options are sold "to close" (i.e., long position is sold), the settlement day is the next business day. The rules concerning the year of recognition are the same as with stock sales as discussed above.

The following table illustrates these rules:

7

Examples of Tax Recognition of Year-End Sales

Stock	Cost	Selling Amount	Gain (Loss)	Date of Sale	Terms	Year Transaction Recognized for Tax Purposes
A	$10	$15	$5	12/30/77	Regular way	1978
B	10	15	5	12/30/77	For cash	1977
C	10	5	(5)	12/30/77	Regular way	1977
D	10	15	5	11/15/77	Deferred delivery (seller's option) — 60 days	1978

Gain or loss on the purchase of stock to close a short sale (settlement five business days after trade date) and on the purchase of a Listed option "to close" the short or written option (settlement one business day after trade date) will be recognized on the settlement date only (see page 59).

Transitional Rule —1978 Year-End Sales

Under the 1978 RA an investor can reduce the effective tax rate on long-term capital gains by postponing his sale of appreciated securities until after October 31, 1978 or until 1979. Where the investor wishes to sell his stock for economic reasons before November 1, 1978 but wants to take advantage of the lower effective long-term capital gains tax rate for post-October 31, 1978 transactions, he should sell short ("short against the box") and close the short sale either in the latter part of 1978 or in 1979. Those investors who have sold property and are receiving the sales proceeds in full or in installments can also benefit from the lowered long-term capital gains rates by arranging to have the payments received after October 31, 1978.

Example: ABC stock is purchased on February 1, 1977 at $20 per share. On October 1, 1978 ABC is selling at $30 per share, but the investor expects the price of the ABC stock to fall. If ABC is sold on October 1, the investor will pay a higher effective tax rate on the capital gains. However, if the ABC stock is sold "short against the box" on October 1, 1978 at $30 per share and the short position is closed in November 1978 or in 1979, the capital gains would be subject to lower tax rates and the seller has avoided any economic risks. (See page 59 for applicable rules.)

An investor who has a large security position with substantial unrealized appreciation and who is negotiating a sale thereof in a private transaction with payment to be spread over a period of years, should consider the availability of the installment sales election of reporting the income realized as a way of deferring the payment of the capital gains tax. Payments in the year of sale must not exceed 30 percent of the selling price. The contract should provide for a minimum of 6 percent annual interest in order to avoid the imputed interest tax provision. Some tender offers, where debt obligations are issued, have been arranged so as to enable the seller to select the installment method of reporting the gain. Note, however, that certain demand obligations or readily tradeable obligations received in corporate acquisitions are treated as cash payments. (See page 119.) An installment sale with the seller's spouse, other family members, or trusts for family members may be permitted under certain circumstances. (See page 132.)

Install-ment Sale of Securities in a Private Transac-tion

An investor in many corporate reorganizations is given the choice of receiving either cash or stock or both in exchange for his stock. Where his stock has appreciated in value, generally it is desirable to receive stock of the acquiring corporation thereby deferring the unrealized gain until a subsequent sale of the stock of the acquiring corporation. If an investor has an unrealized loss on his stock, it may be more beneficial to ask for cash in the exchange and thus recognize the loss in the year of the exchange. Note that if there is a prorata distribution of stock and cash to the shareholders of the acquired corporation in a tax-free reorganization, any loss on the exchange would not be recognized for tax purposes but the receipt of cash may be taxed as a dividend to the extent of any gain.

Tax-Free Reorgani-zation

Holders of certain U.S. Government bonds may have an opportunity to exchange such bonds for other governmental obligations without recognition of gain. The conversion of Series "E" bonds into other government obligations has the effect of deferring the interest element until disposition or redemption of the new bonds. Tax-free exchanges of other types of bonds are also permitted. (See page 119 for discussion dealing with exchange of bonds.)

Exchange of Bonds

A taxpayer can permanently avoid recognition of gain on appreciated securities by giving them to a charity or can substantially avoid tax on the appreciation by selling them to a charity for a price equal to his basis. The charitable contribution deduction in the former situation is the market value, and in the latter case is

Contribu-tion or Bargain Sale of Securities

the difference between market value and the selling price. See page 50 for discussion of the benefits of charitable contribution of low basis appreciated securities.

Offsetting losses In lieu of postponing gain on sale, an investor may prefer to offset the recognized gain by selling other securities at a loss or by entering into other types of transactions. The use of listed options, commodities or other types of options or securities is discussed below. In addition, an investor may prefer to enter into a tax shelter in order to obtain the desired losses. Substantial first year losses can be obtained by entering into cattle or oil transactions. Real estate shelters, on the other hand, will ordinarily throw off deductions over a period of years. However, see page 151 concerning the 1976 TRA and 1978 RA detrimental effect on tax shelters. A long-term capital gain can be offset by a capital loss in a corresponding amount or by an ordinary deduction equal to forty percent of the long-term gain. The use of a capital loss, however, will also reduce the long-term capital gain deduction tax preference for purposes of the alternative minimum tax, but the tax preference will remain if offsetting ordinary deductions are utilized. For example, assume an investor has long-term capital gains of $50,000 and is entitled to a capital gain deduction of $30,000, which is a tax preference item. The remaining taxable gain of $20,000 can be offset by an ordinary deduction of $20,000 thereby eliminating any taxable gain. There will, however, be an outstanding tax preference item of $30,000. If a $50,000 capital loss were realized in the taxable year, the long-term capital gain would be completely eliminated and there would be no tax preference because there would be no long-term capital gain deduction.

INSURE PROPER TIMING AND NATURE OF GAIN OR LOSS

An investor may be in a current security position where some positive action on his part will assure him the desired tax result.

Nature and Timing of Capital Losses Investors should consider taking capital losses within the one year short-term period in order to have the loss sustained carried forward as a short-term loss. Long-term losses sustained are carried forward as long-term losses in succeeding years and must first offset long-term gains in the year to which carried before offsetting short-term gains. (See discussion of capital loss carry-overs on page 62.) It is important where possible to arrange the year's transactions so that long term losses are deductible against short-term gains. To the extent that a capital loss offsets a long-term capital gain after 1978, the average investor is reducing income tax at an effective maximum rate of only 28 percent. By timing to offset the capital losses against short-term gains, the investor is reducing income that may otherwise be subject to an effective maximum rate of 70 percent. (See page 141.)

Example:

	1	2	3	4
Current year long-term gain	$10,000	$10,000	$10,000	—
Current year short-term gain	10,000	10,000	10,000	$10,000
Loss carry-over long-term	—	(10,000)	—	(10,000)
Loss carry-over short-term	—	—	(10,000)	—
Net long-term gain	10,000	—	10,000	—
Net short-term gain	10,000	10,000	—	—
Tax (assume 50% bracket)	$ 7,000	$ 5,000	$ 2,000	—

Tax savings on $10,000 long-term capital loss carry-over (compare Column 1 with Column 2) is $2,000. If the loss carry-over was short-term, such savings would have been $5,000 (compare Column 1 with Column 3). The same savings can be achieved from a long-term loss carry-over (Column 4) only if there are sufficient short-term gains and no long-term gains in the year.

Where part of a position in securities is sold or transferred, adequate identification should be made so as to assure proper and desired tax consequences. (See page 74.)

Identification of Securities

Example:
Position in XYZ Co.:

Date Purchased	Shares	Basis
January 5, 1972	100	$1,000
March 10, 1973	100	3,300
March 15, 1977	100	1,500
September 30, 1978	100	2,800

On December 15, 1978, the investor sells 100 shares for $3,000. By identifying the shares sold, he will recognize either long-term gain (against purchase 1/5/72 or 3/15/77), short-term gain (against purchase 9/30/78) or long-term loss (against purchase 3/10/73). The choice is his. Without proper identification of the certificates delivered, the stock from the 1/5/72 purchase will be deemed the 100 shares sold. (See page 74.)

Worthless Securities —When and How to Take a Loss   It is frequently difficult to establish the worthlessness of a security in order to obtain a deduction. Generally, a sale for more than a nominal amount will show that worthlessness did not occur in an earlier year barred by the statute of limitations for refunds. Because of the difficulty of establishing a worthless deduction it is preferable, where feasible, to sell the stock at a nominal price to an unrelated party, such as a broker. Where the year of worthlessness is in doubt, protective claims for refunds should be filed for each possible year. (See page 121.)

Create Wash Sales   Under certain circumstances it may be desirable to create a wash sale so as to add back to the basis of the newly acquired security, the disallowed loss and holding period. This might be the case where the investor, within 30 days after the sale of securities at a loss, realizes the disadvantageous timing of the capital transactions. (See discussion of Wash Sale Rules, page 77.)

Example (1): T, after holding ABC stock for 8½ months, liquidates his position in 1977 to realize a short-term loss. Subsequently, but within the next 30 days, ABC stock suddenly starts to rise. T now feels that ABC stock has potential appreciation. By repurchasing ABC stock within 30 days after the previous sale, under the wash sale provisions, his loss is not recognized for tax purposes and instead such loss would increase the basis of the new shares acquired. What is more important is that the ABC stock will start off with an 8½ month holding period, thus according sudden substantial overall gain, long-term capital gain treatment by merely holding ABC stock for an additional one-half month period.

Example (2): T, on January 2, 1977 purchased 100 shares of ABC stock at $100 per share (Lot 1) and eight months later on September 2, 1977 purchased an additional 100 shares at $70 per share (Lot 2). By September 20, 1977, ABC has substantially appreciated in value and is selling at $95 per share. If T sells the 200 shares of ABC at $95 per share, he will recognize a net short-term gain of $2,000 ($2,500 gain on Lot 2 less $500 loss on Lot 1).

If instead, T sold 100 shares (Lot 1) on September 20, 1977, the $500 loss sustained is not recognized for tax purposes since T acquired 100 shares of ABC stock (Lot 2) within 30 days prior to such sale. Thus, the $500 loss would increase to $7,500 the basis of the 100 shares acquired on September 1, 1977. More relevant is the new holding period of the remaining 100 shares of ABC stock. The 8 month, 18 day holding period of the Lot 1 shares is added to the 18 day holding period of the Lot 2 100 shares. Thus, for tax purposes, the remaining 100 shares of ABC stock are deemed to have been held for more than nine months and a sale of such shares on the next day, September 21, 1977, for $9,500 will result in the $2,000 net gain being treated as long-term.[3]

Example (3): T sells ABC stock and realizes a short-term loss. Subsequently, he discovers that he would obtain a greater tax benefit if the short-term loss were taken in the next year since he has realized long-term gains in the current year and expects to realize short-term gains in the subsequent year. Therefore, he repurchases the shares within 30 days and resells the stock at a loss in the subsequent year. The short-term loss is then offset against short-term gains and any excess against ordinary income, subject to limitations.

Example (4): In the above example, T realized a long-term loss on the sale which could only be offset against long-term capital gains, or ordinary income at the rate of two dollars of loss for every dollar of ordinary income. By utilizing the wash sales provisions, he can carry the long-term loss into the next year and apply it against short-term gains.

Example (5): T sold ABC stock in December 1978 and realized a short-term loss which would be offset against post-October 31, 1978 long-term gains. He wishes to obtain a 60 percent capital gain deduction on

---

[3] Code: 1223(4)

his long-term capital gains. Accordingly, he washes the loss by repurchasing the stock and then realizes a short-term loss by reselling it in the following year and hopefully will be able to offset it against 1979 short-term gains or against ordinary income.

Example (6): T inadvertently sells shares to a related party and the loss is disallowed under Section 267. (See page 132). Within 30 days he repurchases the shares and later obtains an allowable loss by selling the shares to an unrelated person.

Example (7): T owns 100 shares of ABC stock for several years at $100 per share. ABC stock is currently selling at $40 per share and T wishes to sell his investment and recognize his loss. However the sale would produce a long-term capital loss of $60 per share. If T had sold or written a Listed Call on ABC stock and now purchases the same Call "open" (i.e., creates what is tantamount to a short against the box in Listed options) and within 30 days sells ABC stock for $40 per share, the $6,000 loss would be disallowed under the wash sales rules and would be added to the basis of the Listed Call purchased "open". (The holding period of the option should also include the holding period of the ABC stock. However, this point may be irrelevant.) Thereafter, the long Call is "delivered" against the "short" Call to close. Any gain or loss on the closing of a short Call, under TRA 1976 would be short-term. Accordingly, the $6,000 loss, which otherwise would have been long-term, now may become short-term capital loss (see pages 91 to 103 for full discussion of options and an analysis of the technical and administrative procedures concerning option trading).

Example (8): T has owned 100 shares of ABC stock for several years with a tax basis of $100 per share. T wishes to sell the 100 shares at the current market value of $40 and recognize a $6,000 loss. However, he wishes to convert the loss which otherwise would have been a long-term capital loss into a short-term capital loss. T could purchase a Call on ABC stock at a strike price of 40 and sell the ABC stock at 40. The $6000 loss would be disallowed under the wash sale rules and should be added to the basis of the Call. In addition, the holding period of the stock should also be added to the holding period of the Call. T would exercise the Call and purchase the stock, i.e., ABC stock at $40 per share. The basis of the newly acquired stock would include the basis of the option (i.e., the disallowed loss in the stock sale, $6,000 plus the premium on the Call plus the amount paid for the new stock, $4,000). However, the holding period should completely disappear and thus, the immediate sale of the newly acquired ABC stock would result in a capital loss which should be accorded short-term capital loss treatment. The cost of accomplishing this objective might be too significant, i.e., commission costs on the exercise of the option and on the sale of the second lot of stock and, in addition, the premium paid for the Call.

Example (9): T has owned 100 shares of ABC stock for almost one year with a tax basis of $100 per share. T wishes to maintain his position in ABC stock even though ABC is now selling at $40 per share, but does not wish the potential loss to mature to long-term status. T purchases a Put on ABC stock. It should not matter what the striking price of the Put is nor the duration of the Put, because the mere acquisition of the Put should cause the short sale rules to apply, resulting in the loss of the holding period on the 100 shares of stock. The subsequent disposition of the Put or lapse of the Put will start a new holding period for the stock (see page 86).

Commodity Futures —Create Gain and Loss in Different Taxable Years

Futures in the same commodity but with different delivery dates are not subject to the short sale rules. Thus, a taxpayer can buy and sell short the same commodity with different delivery dates and might be able to create capital gains and losses in different years. (See page 23.) A purchase of a spot commodity contract and a sale of a futures contract with delivery in the following year can result in an ordinary deduction in the current year and long-term gains in the next year. (See page 32). A purchase and sale of Treasury bills may result in an ordinary deduction in the current year and ordinary income in the next year. (See pages 32 and 109.)

Obligations Issued at a Discount

An investor may elect in any taxable year to include in income annually the increase in the redemption value of certain non-interest bearing obligations issued at a discount, such as Series "E" savings bonds. Thus, if it is advantageous to increase income of a given year, the election can be made. If an election is not made during his lifetime, it can be made on the deceased investor's final return. (See page 46.)

(See page 46.)

Sale of Municipal Bonds at a Loss

Many tax-exempt bonds are selling far below their original offering price because of the increase in interest rates since the tax-exempt bonds were issued. Holders of these bonds have the choice of selling them at a loss or holding them until maturity and receiving the face value of the bonds upon redemption. A sale of these bonds gives the investor not only a capital loss which can be offset against capital gains and to a limited extent against income, but also provides an opportunity to upgrade the investments or purchase bonds with proportionately higher yields. For example, T purchased $10,000 of 3% municipal bonds which mature in 1987 and which are presently selling at 80, or $8,000 for all of the bonds. By selling the bonds T would recognize a $2,000 capital loss. The proceeds are then reinvested in 6% tax-exempts thereby increasing the tax-free interest yield from $300 to $480. The current use of the capital loss plus the increased interest yield may more than offset the loss of $2,000 upon redemption of the bonds at maturity. Note that the wash sales rules do not apply to the losses where securities which are not substantially identical are acquired.

PROTECT APPRECIATION ON LONG-TERM POSITION WITH POSSIBILITY OF ADDITIONAL LONG-TERM CAPITAL GAINS

If the investor has held a profitable position for more than one year and wants to protect the long-term capital gain, he may consider selling the stock short-against-the-box and simultaneously purchasing a Call. Thus, for the cost of a Call, he is both ensuring his present economic gain and will also obtain the benefit of any future appreciation in the stock.

> *Example:* T, on June 1, 1977, purchased 100 shares of ABC stock at $20. On June 2, 1978 ABC stock is selling at $30. T could buy one Jan. ABC 30 at $3 ($300) and sell short 100 shares of ABC at $30. If ABC declines below $30 by the middle of January 1979,

16

the long position could be delivered against the short position resulting in a $1,000 long-term capital gain, and the worthless Call would result in a $300 short-term capital loss. If ABC should rise to $50, the 100 share long position could be sold, resulting in $3,000 long-term capital gain, and a $300 long-term capital loss would result under the short sale rules on the exercise of the Call and delivery of the stock to close the short position. The net long-term capital gain would be $2,700. Thus, T was able to insure a minimum long-term capital gain at a cost of $300, and, if successful, as in the example, obtain an additional economic gain of $1,700 for a total of $2,700 of long-term capital gain.

CONVERT SHORT-TERM GAIN INTO LONG-TERM GAIN

Investors owning appreciated securities or options for less than one year may wish to protect their economic gain and still maintain their position in order to have the recognized gain treated as long-term. The ensuing transactions may accomplish this objective.

Sale of Call on Appreciated Long Position

An investor who has owned appreciated stock for less than one year can sell a Call on the stock which will not expire until the stock has been held for more than one year. The investor will thus give the purchaser of the Call an option to acquire the investor's stock at a specific price within a specified period of time. If the stock should have a further moderate increase in value, and the Call is exercised toward the end of its term, the investor will be assured of long-term capital gain to the extent that the Call price plus the amount received on the sale of the Call exceeds the basis of the stock. If the stock has substantially increased in value, the investor could buy other shares of the stock in the open market to deliver against the Call or, if dealing in Listed Calls, buy the Call long in a closing transaction, recognize a short-term loss, and sell his long position for greater long-term gain. Due to the increased holding period requirements, the Call period may also have to be for a longer duration to ensure long-term capital gain treatment.

> *Example:* T acquires 100 shares of ABC on 2/1/77 at $10 per share. On 12/18/77 ABC is selling at $30 per

share. T sells a Listed Call in ABC at $30 due 2/18/78 for the equivalent of $2 per share ($200). If the ABC stock is selling on or about 2/17/78 at slightly above $30, the holder of the Call will exercise it and T will recognize a long-term capital gain of $22 per share ($30 plus $2 less $10). If ABC stock is selling at $40, T would buy the Listed Call to close for approximately $1000, the equivalent of $10 per share, thus recognizing a short-term capital loss of $8 per share. He could also sell his long position with a basis of $10 for $40, recognizing a long-term gain of $30. His net economic gain is still $22, but $30 is long-term gain and $8 is short-term loss.

If the market value of the stock should fall, the investor is economically protected to the extent of the premium received on the Call, which would be taxed as a short-term gain (a lapse of a Call written before September 1, 1976 resulted in ordinary income). Under the facts in the example, an investor in the 50 percent tax bracket will realize greater economic gain after taxes by waiting for a more than one year holding period before selling, provided that ABC stock stays above $22 (long-term gain of at least $12 netting $9 plus $1 of after-tax income on $2 proceeds from the sale of the Call, is equivalent to the $20 of short-term gain which would have been realized from a sale at $30). Thus unless there is a substantial break in the market, the investor will be assured of some long-term capital gain with a hedge against a decline to the extent of the premium received on the sale of the Call.

If the Call is sold initially at a price below the market, ("in the money") the investor will increase the chances that the Call will be exercised, so that the increased premium for writing the more valuable Call will be given long-term capital gain treatment. Thus, in the example above, if a Listed Call on ABC at $20 were being traded, it probably would be selling close to its intrinsic value of $10 per share with very little additional premium, if any, for the time value. Assuming a selling price equivalent to $10 per share ($1,000), T, by writing such an "in the money" Listed Call, will be assured of exercise and long-term capital gain (on the assumption of exercise after February 1, 1978) as long as the stock remains above $20 per share.

The investor may take advantage of the current market price and still prolong his holding period for up to 60 days. This is accomplished by selling at today's market price, and contracting that payment and delivery will take place on a specified date within 60 days following the date of contract, with all dividends to stockholders of record before the delivery date belonging to the seller. Special arrangements must be made to have the dividends accrue to the seller. Otherwise under the normal deferred delivery transaction, dividends payable after the contract date would go to the buyer which might affect the rule as to when the sale takes place. The intent of the parties is that title passes on the delivery date. Thus, an investor who has a holding period of between ten months and one year could convert unrealized short-term gain into long-term gain without any economic risk. It is understood that the Treasury's position in such a case is that the contract date is not regarded as controlling, and that the sale does not take place until the delivery date. A slight reduction in sales price is generally required to obtain a purchaser for deferred delivery stock.

Deferred Delivery under NYSE Rule 64(3) (Seller's Option)

> *Example:* T acquired XYZ stock on February 1, 1978 at $30 per share. On December 15, 1978 the market value has risen to $64 at which time T wishes to liquidate his position and thereby protect his gain. By selling on a deferred delivery basis, for delivery on February 2, 1979, usually at a $1 to $2 discount (assuming no usual dividend record date falls in the interim), T will recognize in 1979 long-term gain of approximately $32 per share ($62 discounted selling price less $30 cost) in lieu of recognizing $34 short-term gain per share in 1978. T, who is in the 50 percent tax bracket, will earn in after-tax dollars, $24 per share under the deferred delivery sale, in lieu of $17 per share had he sold the stock in the regular way on December 15, 1978.

Where an investor has held a long-term Unlisted Call for less than one year, he may economically protect himself against a decline in the market by selling short a comparable number of shares of the underlying stock. If after the one year holding period, the Call is still appreciated, he can sell the Call, recognizing long-term gain, and close out the short sale, recognizing short-term gain or loss. In the event the market continues to rise after the short sale, a sale of the Call after the one year holding period will result in an

Selling Short Against Appreciated Calls to Insure Gain

increased long-term capital gain and the closing of the short position would create a short-term loss. In any event the investor has locked in his economic profit. The Call and the underlying stock are not considered substantially identical so as to come within the short sale rules.[4] (See page 87.)

> *Example:* T acquires on March 1, 1977, a one-year, ten-day Unlisted Call on 100 shares of ABC stock at $30 per share for a cost of $400. On February 1, 1978, ABC stock is selling at $50. By selling short 100 shares at $50, T is assured of economic gain of at least $1,600 ($5,000 short sale amount less a cost of $3,000 for the stock if purchased and $400 for the Call). Assume that on March 1, 1978, ABC stock is selling at $70. T would sell the Call for approximately $4,000 (difference between market value of $70 per share and the Call price of $30 per share), recognizing $3,600 of long-term gain (after deducting cost of $400 for the Call). T would sustain a short-term loss of $2,000 on the closing of the short sale. His economic pre-tax gain is still $1,600. If the ABC stock had instead been selling at $15 on March 1, T would realize $3,500 short-term gain on the closing of the short sale, a long-term loss of $400 on the expiration of the Call (loss would be short-term if the Call were sold prior to the one-year holding period), for a net economic gain of $3,100.

Commodity Straddles

Due to the increased holding period for long-term gains, there will be more short-term capital gains realized by investors. The cost of acquiring Unlisted Calls or other options for more than one year will be a good deal more expensive than purchasing shorter term Calls. Furthermore, gains realized by writers of Listed options will now normally be short-term capital gains. Note, that any type of commodity future, whether it be bullion or agricultural, retains the more than six-month period for long-term capital gain. Therefore, instead of artificially changing a normal investment transaction in order to obtain long-term capital gains, often at great expense, the utilization of the commodity straddle as an investment vehicle in order to take advantage of positive economic

---

[4] Rev. Rul. 58-384, C.B. 1958-2, 410

factors, may also result in the conversion of short-term gains into long-term gains (see pages 23 and 105).

CONVERT CAPITAL LOSS INTO ORDINARY DEDUCTION

An investor may have incurred a substantial capital loss and does not expect to realize offsetting capital gains in the near future. The capital loss may be offset against ordinary income, within limitations, but it may take many years before the investor could fully utilize the capital loss in this manner. He may be of advanced age and there may be a good likelihood that he will die before obtaining the full benefit of his capital loss. Any unused capital loss would expire with his demise. In addition, if the loss is long-term, it would require $2 of the long-term loss to offset $1 of ordinary income, so that the investor would in effect lose the benefit of one half his loss. A capital gain created to offset the large capital loss would result, in effect, in "tax-free income", while the ordinary deduction would offset ordinary income.

Cash and Carry Commodity Transaction

A capital gain to offset the large capital loss can be created by purchasing a spot commodity contract and selling a commodity future contract at a greater sales price. The commodity received on the spot contract would be stored in a warehouse and the warehousing expense and interest charge incurred in borrowing to carry the commodity are deductible against ordinary income. Upon closing the futures contracts, the investor would realize a short-term capital gain that would be offset against the capital loss (see page 26 for detailed explanation).

Commodity Straddle

By buying and selling commodity futures with different settlement dates, the investor could close his profitable position in the current year and offset the realized short-term gain against the long-term capital loss. At the beginning of the next year he would close-out his loss position and realize a short-term loss. (See page 24 for detailed example.) This short-term loss would be offset against subsequent short-term gains or, subject to limitations, against ordinary income on a $1 to $1 basis. This alternative is not as advantageous as the "cash and carry" alternative because the short-term loss may not be fully utilized in the near future. The costs of entering into a commodity straddle plus the possibility of an economic loss should be considered before adopting this alternative. See also the chapter on "Create Capital Gain and Ordinary Deduction", starting on page 26, for other possible alternatives.

CREATE LONG-TERM GAIN AND SHORT-TERM LOSS

The ensuing transactions may create the desired short-term capital loss which will offset existing short-term capital gains, or short-term capital gains created from naked or covered option writing (see page 26), cash and carry commodity transactions (see page 26), or other similar transactions, and simultaneously create the desired long-term capital gain.

Arbitraging Securities Not Substantially Identical

Long-term capital gains can be obtained in arbitrage situations if the long position is held open for more than one year and if the securities sold short are not "substantially identical" to the long securities for purposes of the short sale rules. (See page 87.)

Example: X and Y corporations plan to merge and the stock of X corporation will be exchanged evenly for shares of Y corporation. Prior to approval by the shareholders, the two securities are not considered to be substantially identical. (See page 87.) X stock is selling at $20 and Y stock is selling at $22. The investor buys X stock and sells Y stock short. It is immaterial that the X stock subsequently becomes "substantially identical" to the Y stock.[5] It should also be immaterial that after an exchange for X stock, Y stock is now held in a long position. The exchange should not be deemed an acquisition of the Y stock bringing into play the short sale rules. (See page 83.)

The closing of the long position of the Y stock received in the exchange against the short position of Y after the requisite one year holding period will result in long-term gain to the extent of the

[5] Rev. Rul. 62-153, C.B. 1962-2, 186

initial spread of $2 per share. If the value of Y stock at the time of delivery rises above $22 per share, then the Y stock received on the exchange should be sold in order to recognize long-term capital gains greater than the initial spread of $2 per share. The short position should be covered through the purchase in the open market of Y stock, resulting in the recognition of a short-term capital loss which could be utilized to offset short-term capital gains. The net economic gain will be equal to the initial spread of $2 per share, but the character of the gain and loss for tax purposes will be different.

Commodity Futures The purchase and short sale of the same commodity future calling for delivery in different months are not within the short sale rules. (See page 83.) The investor may avail himself of this statutory exception, when entering into this transaction for profit, to establish a long-term gain and an approximately equivalent short-term loss, where such is desired. In addition, the investor may create capital gains and losses in different years so as to offset unwanted capital gains or losses previously realized during the year. Thus, an investor who realized short-term gains because of the increased holding period rules or the restrictive rules for writers of options, might still convert the gain into long-term by subsequently entering into commodity straddles. On the other hand, an investor, with capital losses or expiring net operating losses, might close out his profitable position in the current taxable year and defer his capital loss (preferably short term) until the subsequent year. The six-month holding period for long-term capital gains has been retained for commodity futures. (See page 106.)

However, the Internal Revenue Service has ruled that the short-term capital loss generated in a silver straddle transaction very similar to Example (b) that follows, results in no real economic loss and is not deductible.[6] The government's ruling seems erroneous since its position fails to recognize the total economics and profit potential of commodity straddle transactions. A drop in interest rates will cause the spread between the contracts to narrow resulting in significant potential gain on the facts indicated in Example (b). In fact, sometimes an inversion occurs, whereby

---

[6]Rev. Rul. 77-185, I.R.B. 1977-21, 7

the further out silver future will fall in price below the nearer term silver future resulting in significant overall pre-tax profit.

Example (a): *Long-term gain and short-term loss:* On June 1, 1977, T enters into a contract to buy 5,000 ounces of March 1978 silver and at the same time enters into a contract to sell 5,000 ounces of May 1978 silver. More than six months later, on December 2, 1977, assume both futures have risen in value by 50 cents an ounce (normally the price movement of each part of the straddle changes separately causing significant economic potential, i.e., profit or loss). T, by closing out each contract separately, will realize a long-term capital gain of $2,500 on the long position of March 1978 silver and a $2,500 short-term capital loss on the short sale of May 1978 silver. (Gain or loss recognized on the closing of a short position in commodity futures will always be short-term no matter how long the position is kept open.) The market price of futures having different maturity dates will not necessarily fluctuate proportionately. However, the proportionate fluctuations in prices tend to be closer as the maturity dates are more distant in time. A careful study must be made of the particular commodity future to be used in the transaction to determine the possibilities of economic gain or loss. It is possible that the transaction may result in an economic loss which could outweigh the tax advantage.

If both futures have declined in value, T should close out the long position before his holding period is more than six months in order to prevent the loss from becoming long-term. The closing of both contracts prior to such six-month holding period, except for differences in fluctuations of price, will result in almost a complete wash of gain and loss, both being short-term.

Example (b): *Create capital gains and losses in different years:* T has large short-term gains realized in the current taxable year. The use of commodity futures will enable him to recognize loss in one year, with comparable gain in the next year, and be subjected to little market risk.

T could enter into the transaction described in (a) above in November of 1977. Assuming that the market value of silver rises in value by 50 cents an ounce, T would close out his short position in May 1978 silver by December 31, 1977, recognizing a short-term loss of $2,500.

He immediately would sell short July 1978 silver in order to be protected against a decline of silver futures. In the subsequent year, both the March 1978 long position and July 1978 short position would be sold with a resulting net short-term gain approximately equivalent to the $2,500 short-term loss recognized in December 1977. Similar action on the part of T in case of market decline will accomplish the same results.

It is possible under the transactions described in (a) and (b) above to defer paying tax on the short-term gains realized in the earlier year and also convert the gains into long-term gains in the succeeding year, provided there is a rise in the market value of the future and there is sufficient time left before the maturity dates of the contracts to accomplish the latter objective.

Acquisition of Shares in a Mutual Fund

An investor in a high tax bracket and having large short-term capital gains would welcome the opportunity to create short-term capital losses and long-term capital gains, and thereby convert his realized short-term capital gains into long-term capital gains. The investor should consider buying shares in a mutual fund immediately prior to a large capital gain distribution, hold the mutual fund for more than 31 days and then liquidate his position.[7] The market value of the fund will drop approximately equivalent to the amount of the capital gain distribution if there is no other change in the value of the assets of the fund for the 31-day period. The investor will treat the capital gains distribution as long-term and the loss on the sale of the fund as short-term. However, the investor is subjected to the vagaries of the market for the 31-day period. The "loading" charges of some mutual funds would increase the loss on the sale to such an extent as to make this device uneconomic. However, shares of so-called "no-load" funds may be available. Shares of a "close-end" mutual fund could also be utilized in a similar manner; however, a commission expense will be incurred upon acquisition and subsequent sale of such shares.

[7] Code section 852(b)(4) necessitates a 31-day holding period; otherwise the loss on sales of the stock would be treated as long-term.

Example: T purchases on November 15, 1977, 1,000 shares of ABC Fund (a no-load fund) for $20 per share. ABC Fund distributes a $2 long-term capital gain dividend. T will recognize long-term capital gains on the receipt of the $2,000 distribution even though he has held ABC stock for merely one day. The value of ABC Fund will fall to $18 per share. Assuming that there are no changes in the value of ABC Fund for the next 31 days, T would sell the 1,000 shares after December 16, 1977 and realize a $2,000 short-term capital loss (cost of $20,000 less selling amount of $18,000).

CREATE CAPITAL GAIN AND ORDINARY DEDUCTION

Certain forms of investments discussed below, by their component steps and tax treatment, create capital gain and ordinary deduction. Many investors have avoided these types of investments because of apparent complexities and often-times undesired short-term capital gain results. However, sophisticated investors have realized that the pure economics, i.e., the profit potential, is overriding, and have accepted these forms of investments as the most desirable from a risk-reward viewpoint. They have looked to additional types of investments such as the commodity straddle transactions (see page 23) to offset the short-term capital gains and create long-term capital gains.

Sometimes the separate tax treatment of each component of these transactions can be beneficial to the taxpayer without any further transactions. For example, investors with substantial capital loss carryovers will effectively have the short-term capital gain treated as tax-free income.

Cash and Carry Commodity Transaction

A capital gain and ordinary deduction can be created by purchasing a spot commodity contract and selling a commodity future contract at a greater sales price. The investor hopes to make money in this transaction due to expectations of changes in interest rates, possible lock-in of "positive interest carry", or potential closing of the spread (or even the inversion thereof) between the spot price and the future price. (See page 109 for more details.) The commodity received on the spot contract would be stored in a warehouse and the warehousing expense and interest charge incurred in borrowing to carry the commodity are deductible against ordinary income. Upon closing the futures contract, the investor would realize a capital gain (generally short-term, unless the commodity was held for more than one year).

Example: T purchases on May 1, 1977 20,000 ounces of silver at $4.80 per ounce and sells 4 contracts of July 1978 silver at $5.22 per ounce. As indicated in the illustration (see page 29), based upon the assumptions used, T will have a pre-tax profit of $1,200 and an after-tax profit of $2,900. Several observations concerning the illustration are relevant:

1. The pre-tax profit will vary depending upon the relationship of the cost of financing (i.e., $6\frac{1}{2}\%$) when compared to the spread between the spot price and the future price (i.e., $5.22 − $4.80 = $.42 spread per ounce). Note that a cash and carry transaction would not be valid for tax purposes if the interest rates are so high that the investor could not under reasonable circumstances realize an economic gain.

2. In lieu of cash, U.S. Treasury bills are accepted as original margin on the sale of July 1978 silver (minimum face amount of $10,000). Fluctuations in the price of the futures contract will result in changes in margin requirements (variation margin).

3. A shorter-term futures contract could be sold, causing the locked-in spread to be treated as short-term capital gain. (The holding period of the spot silver must be more than one year, as in the illustration, to be accorded long-term capital gain treatment.) A simultaneous commodity straddle transaction in silver futures could be created to defer the gain into a subsequent year and convert it into long-term capital gain (see page 23).

4. The relationship between the ordinary income tax bracket and long-term capital gain tax bracket (60% vs. 30% in the illustration) and potential minimum and maximum tax effects (see page 141) must be considered.

5. Normally the earlier month commodity future is purchased (e.g., on April 15, 1977 T could buy 4 contracts of May 1977 silver selling at $4.80 per ounce and delivery of the actual silver would occur early in the following month).

6. The investor should not enter into the spot commodity transaction in a jurisdiction where a sales tax liability might be applicable to the gross purchase amount.

Covered Option Writing

Covered option writing (i.e., writing one Call for each 100 shares of stock owned or, in the alternative, writing one Put for each 100 shares of stock sold short) may result in a reduction of risk of loss under adverse market conditions and increased economic yield on his investment position. Covered option writing on a fully margined basis will tend to further increase the economic yield under stable or positive market conditions and will create larger capital gains and larger interest expense deductions. (See page 91 for detailed discussion of options).

Example: On September 30, 1977, T purchases 1000 shares of ABC stock at $28½ and writes 10 ABC Calls, Jan. 25's, for a premium of $650 each ($6½ per share) or a total of $6,500. Thus, T is selling to an investor the right to purchase 1,000 shares of ABC stock at $25 per share any time between September 30, 1977 and January 21, 1978. The intrinsic value of the Call is $3½ per share (the difference between $28½ fair market value and $25 striking price of the Call), and the balance of the premium of the Call of $3 per share represents the time value portion. Assuming no change in price of the underlying stock, the time value generally diminishes as the Call approaches expiration. Disregarding commission expense, the maximum economic gain that T could realize, which will occur as long as ABC stock stays at or above $25 per share, is $3,000, which will be short-term capital gain in 1978, if the Call is exercised after December 29, 1977. This amount will be reduced by the interest cost on the borrowed funds of $14,250 by approximately $400, most of which will be deducted in 1977. The net cash amount invested by T is approximately $8,000 (50% of $28,500, less the Call premium of $6,500). T cannot incur an economic loss unless

ILLUSTRATION—CASH AND CARRY TRANSACTION

Calculation of Pre-Tax Profit or Loss
May 1, 1977

Purchase 20,000 Troy ozs. silver @ $4.80 per oz.	$ 96,000	
Bank financing—90% of value of silver	(86,400)	
Margin on sale of 4 contracts July 1978 silver @ $5.22 per oz.	4,000	
Estimated Commissions	100	
Carrying charges—Bank interest $86,400 @ 6½% for 14 months	6,600	
Storage @ 25¢ per 5,000 oz. lot per day (4 lots x 425 days x 25¢)	400	
Total Cash Required		$20,700

July 1, 1978

Deliver 20,000 oz. in settlement of sales contract @ $5.22 per oz.	$104,400	
Commissions	(100)	
Repayment of bank loan	(86,400)	
Return of margin	4,000	
Total cash proceeds		$21,900
Net cash profit before tax consequences		$ 1,200

Calculation of Income Tax Consequences
   1977 and 1978 Ordinary Loss

Interest	$ 6,600	
Storage	400	
Total	$ 7,000	
Tax Savings @ 60%		$ 4,200

1978 Long-Term Capital Gain on Delivery

Proceeds ($104,400 − $100)	$104,300	
Cost ($ 96,000 + $100)	96,100	
Long-Term Capital Gain	$ 8,200	
Tax cost @ 30%		($ 2,500)
NET TAX BENEFIT		$ 1,700
TOTAL AFTER-TAX PROFIT		$ 2,900

ABC stock falls below $22 per share ($28½ cost less option premium of $6½). The amount of the time value premium is a function of the volatility of the underlying stock (period of time to expiration and the relationship of intrinsic value to total premium). Generally, as the intrinsic value increases, the time premium will shrink, irrespective of time to expiration.

If the Call should expire unexercised, (i.e., ABC stock is selling below $25), the $6,500 premium will be short-term capital gain in 1978. If ABC stock is also sold (e.g., sold at $24 per share), the resulting loss will be a short-term capital loss of $4,500.

If ABC should rise to $40 per share, T may wish to buy, in a closing transaction, the ABC Jan. 25's for the equivalent of $15 per share ($15,000 for 10 Calls) and recognize a short-term capital loss of $8,500. T could write higher striking price and longer duration ABC Calls (e.g., Oct. 35's) with a view towards obtaining additional yield and maturing his stock position for long-term capital gain potential.

Options written prior to September 2, 1976 were accorded ordinary income or loss treatment on a closing transaction or if the Call lapsed unexpired. The only Listed options were Calls. Thus, in the above situation, the $8,500 loss would have been ordinary loss under the prior law.

Treasury Bills, Treasury Bill Futures, and Options on Treasury Bills and Treasury Bill Futures

Because of the restrictions placed on Listed options and tax shelters by the 1976 TRA, some investors have turned to Treasury bills and Treasury bill futures as a means of obtaining an ordinary deduction and capital gains. (See page 110 for discussion as to whether Treasury bill futures constitute a capital asset and how an ordinary loss can be obtained in any event.)

Example (1): T establishes a Treasury bill spread, i.e., purchases the Jan. 10, 1978 treasury bills and sells the Feb. 7, 1978 short. The nature of the Treasury bills, since they are discounted paper, is that, at the expiration of a period of time, a loss will be realized in the short position with a corresponding "gain" on the long position. Accordingly, T will buy in the short position to establish an ordinary loss and resell another short position to continue the hedge. In the subsequent year both positions will be terminated. The resulting net gain will be ordinary income. The economics of the transaction are that the one-month spread between the long and short position can produce income, provided interest rates rise. In the alternative, a loss will be sustained if interest rates decline. In addition, a change in the yield curve could have significant economic effect.

Example (2): In lieu of establishing a long position in Treasury bills, T could in Example 1 purchase Treasury bill futures as his long position which are traded on a listed exchange. However, a hedge would not be established. Instead, gain or loss on the futures contract will depend upon changes in the yield rate. It is arguable that the gain sustained on the Treasury bill futures will be capital gain (see page 110). Thus, if the position could have been held for more than 12 months, the gain would have been long-term capital gain. It may be further contended that a Treasury bill future might be considered to be a commodity traded on a listed exchange and accordingly, only the six month holding period would be required to establish long-term capital gain.

Any short-term gain generated on this spread might be converted into a long-term gain by means of a commodity straddle (see page 23). Because of the unclear tax treatment, an investor should be wary about entering into such transactions until Treasury approval is obtained. Note that approval would not be necessary if trading in options on on Treasury bills commences. Ordinary income or loss would result on the disposition of the long options, while short-term capital gain or loss would result upon the disposition of the "short" option (see page 110).

A simple means of deferring ordinary income can be obtained by purchasing a large quantity of Treasury bills on margin. An interest deduction can be taken in the current year and the Treasury bill income is not reportable until the bills mature in the following year. Repurchase agreements, executed on a 30 day basis, with longer term Treasuries might be the only way to show a potential economic profit on the assumption that interest rates remain constant.

Selling Short before Ex-Dividend Date

An investor intending to establish a short position should enter into the short sale before the ex-dividend date in order to obtain an ordinary deduction for the amount paid as a dividend on the short sale and thus have the resulting equivalent amount potentially available as capital gain. (However, if the dividend is a stock dividend or liquidating dividend, the Treasury will not allow the deduction.) Generally the market value of the stock on the ex-dividend date falls in an amount equal to the dividend paid. If the investor subsequently covers his short position and there is no other variation in the value of the stock, he will realize a short-term capital gain approximately equivalent to the amount paid as a dividend on the short sale. The same possibility may exist with respect to selling short a flat bond where a significant arrearage interest will be made in the near future. A short-term gain might be desired in order to offset short-term losses that would otherwise offset long-term gains. However, it should be noted that where the sole purpose of the transaction is tax avoidance, the deductibility of the dividend paid may be questioned. (See page 130.)

Example (1): ABC stock is scheduled to go ex-dividend a $1 dividend on December 15, 1977; T wishes to sell the stock short at $60. If he establishes the short position prior to December 15, 1977, he will have to pay $1 per share for such dividend, for which he becomes entitled to a $1 per share ordinary deduction. Assuming no other changes in market value, ABC stock should fall in price to $59 thereby creating a potential short-term gain of $1 per share. However, if T waits until December 15, 1977, he will establish his short position at a price of $59 per share, the market value on that day. T will not have any ordinary deduction, nor the built-in potential capital gain of $1 per share.

Example (2): ABC 6½% Debentures are trading flat at $112. An arrearage interest payment of 2½ years or $16.25 will be paid on June 1, 1977. T wishes to sell the debenture short on the assumption that the debenture, after the interest payment, will fall in price more than $16.25. Assuming no other changes in market value, ABC Debenture should decrease in price to $95.75 thereby creating a potential short-term gain of $162.50 per $1,000 bond. T will have to pay $162.50 per $1,000 bond on the short side which should be an ordinary deduction (see page 130).

Holders of taxable bonds which are selling at a premium and have appreciated in value, for example, because of changes in the going interest rate, should sell the bonds, and immediately repurchase an equal number of the same bonds. Gains on the sale of the bonds held for more than one year are taxed at the lower capital gains rate. The premium paid on the subsequent repurchase (not attributable to any conversion privilege) may be deducted against ordinary income through amortization usually computed to the maturity date.[8] (See page 112.)

Sale and Repurchase of Appreciated Bonds

> *Example:* T owns $50,000 of 10% noncallable and nonconvertible XYZ bonds due January 1, 1982 which he acquired at par in 1975. These bonds on January 2, 1977 are selling at 105 and are therefore worth $52,500. If T sells these bonds, he will recognize a long-term capital gain of $2,500. Assuming he still wants to maintain his investment position in these bonds, he would repurchase them at 105 for $52,500. T should then elect to amortize the $2,500 premium over the remaining term of the bonds. Thus, T would be entitled to a deduction against ordinary income of $500 per year ($2,500 amortized over the period of 1977 through 1982). T, in the 50 percent tax bracket, may pay a capital gain tax of $625 in 1977, but would have available ordinary deductions each year which might result in tax savings of $250 annually or $1,250 over the five-year period.

When interest rates are at high levels, many high grade low interest rate bonds will be selling at substantial discounts. Investors who anticipate a decline in the interest rates are in a position to make substantial gains by purchasing these deep discount bonds on the highest margin available. The interest income on these bonds is taxable at ordinary income rates, but the spread between the purchase price and the amount received on sale or redemption is taxed at capital gain rates. The interest paid on the bank loans is

Deep Discount Bonds

[8] Rev. Rul. 55-353, C.B. 1955-1, 381

deductible (see page 125 for discussion of limitations on investment interest expense) against ordinary income. Moreover, the higher the income tax bracket of the investor, the greater will be his after-tax gain. This type of transaction was even more attractive if the interest expense was prepaid, but a current deduction for prepayment is no longer permitted.

Example: T, in the 50 percent bracket, purchases on February 1, 1977, $100,000 of XYZ 4% bonds due February 1, 1982 at 80, which is financed by a bank loan for $80,000 at 9 percent interest. Assuming the bonds are redeemed at par at maturity, the following are the pre-tax and after-tax results:

	Pre-Tax Results		After-Tax Results	
Interest Income	$20,000		$10,000	
Gain on redemption	20,000	$40,000	16,000	$26,000
Less: Interest paid	36,000		18,000	
Commissions	250	36,250	200	18,200
Net Gain		$ 3,750		$ 7,800

Nondividend Paying Stock Long-term gain and ordinary deduction can also be obtained by purchasing on margin nondividend paying stock of a corporation which plows all of the corporate profits back into the business. The average investor can deduct the interest paid on the margin and pay capital gains tax on sale of the stock. (See page 125 for discussion of limitations on the deductibility of investment interest expense.)

Example: On January 2, 1978 T purchases on 50 percent margin 100 shares of ABC stock for $50,000. T pays the maximum amount of deductible interest in 1978 and deducts this amount in the year paid. On January 3, 1979 the stock has appreciated in value to $60,000 and T sells the stock and pays a capital gains tax on the $10,000 gain.

Tax Shelters Certain types of tax shelters can also generate ordinary deductions and capital gains upon disposition. Real estate investments can still produce losses during the early years (but there are transitional rules limiting construction period deductions) and a gain on sale will be treated as capital gains after first recapturing certain depreciation in excess of straight-line depreciation. An oil and gas investment will throw off larger deductions in the first year, but under the new rules gain on a subsequent sale will be treated as ordinary income to the extent of excess intangible drilling expenses. Investing in a breeder cattle program for a period of approximately five years will also result in ordinary deductions in the early years and capital gains primarily from the sale of cattle born after commencement of the cattle breeder program. (See page 151 for a more detailed discussion of the effect of the 1976 TRA on tax shelters.) One of the benefits of tax shelters is that income generally will be deferred for a longer period of time than through the use of securities or commodities. The economic risks involved, the costs of entering into the transaction, and the capital requirements must also be considered before a decision is reached as to the best type of investment to accomplish the desired economic and tax goals.

OBTAIN LONG-TERM GAINS IN A DECLINING MARKET—ACQUISITION OF A PUT IN LIEU OF SELLING SHORT

If the investor is bearish with regard to a particular stock, he should consider the purchase of a one-year, ten-day (or longer term) Unlisted Put in lieu of selling the stock short. In the event his expectations of a falling market are realized, he may sell the Put just prior to its expiration (or after a one-year hold period), recognizing long-term gain. (See pages 36 and 94.) The investor's gain will be lower as compared to a short sale of the stock (by the cost of the Put), but the gain will be taxed at substantially lower rates. On the other hand, had the investor sold the stock short, any gain on the closing of the short sale would be short-term. (See pages 83 to 91.) If the stock should rise in price, the investor should sell the Put prior to the one-year holding period in order to have the loss sustained treated as short-term. (See page 94). His loss would be limited to the cost of the Put. However, with a short sale, his loss could be substantially greater. In view of the fact that the amount of funds necessary to acquire a Put may be substantially less than the funds necessary to margin a short sale, greater economic leverage may be obtained by acquiring a Put. The economic leverage may be further increased through the acquisition of a "discounted Put" (the option price of the stock is below the current market price) at a substantially reduced cost, but with the potential profit also reduced to the extent of the discount. The cost of acquiring a Put for more than one year in order to obtain long-term capital gain treatment is more expensive than the previous requirement of a six-month holding period. There are also additional risks that prices will increase because of the extended holding period, but on the other hand the investor will also have a greater period of time to fulfill his expectations and he can sell or exercise his Put, if required, before the requisite one-year holding period is met.

> *Example:* T expects XYZ stock selling at $30 per share to fall in price. T purchases a one-year, ten-day Unlisted Put for $400, which gives him the right to sell 100 shares of XYZ stock at $30 during the term of the option. Assume that at the end of one year, XYZ stock is selling for $20. T would then sell the Put for approximately $1,000, realizing a net long-term gain of $600 ($1,000 less the $400 cost of the Put). If T had sold short 100 shares of XYZ stock, he would have realized approximately $1,000 economic gain which would be treated as short-term.
>
> If T were in the 60 percent tax bracket, the long-term gain of $600 would produce $450 in after-tax income while the short-term gain of $1,000 would produce $400 in after-tax income. If XYZ stock had instead risen to $50 at the end of the one-year period, T would sustain only a $400 short-term loss (assuming he had sold the Put just prior to the one-year holding period) as compared to a $2,000 short-term loss had he sold short 100 shares of XYZ stock. T's investment in the Put would be lower if he acquired a discounted Put, e.g., $300 for a Put on XYZ stock at $27 where the market value of the stock was $30 per share.

OBTAIN LONG-TERM GAINS ON
APPRECIATED OPTIONS

Sale of a Call or Put Held for More than One Year Where the investor holds an Unlisted Call, which has appreciated in value, for more than one year, and he does not wish to maintain an interest in the stock, the Call should be sold in order to convert the recognized gain into a long-term gain. If the Call is exercised and the underlying stock is sold within one year, the resulting gain would constitute a short-term gain. (See page 97.)

Similar action should be taken with respect to an Unlisted Put held for more than one year. Although the acquisition of a Put is considered a short sale for purposes of applying the short sale rules, under other tax provisions dealing with options the Put is treated as a capital asset in the hands of the investor and its sale results in long- or short-term capital gain or loss depending upon the holding period.

> *Example:* An investor on June 1, 1977 purchased a one-year, ten-day Unlisted Call on 100 shares of XYZ stock at $30 per share for $400. On June 2, 1978 XYZ stock is selling at $50 per share. The investor should sell the Call in lieu of exercising it and then sell the stock. The sale of the Call will produce a long-term capital gain of approximately $1,600, while the sale of the stock received on exercise of the Call will result in approximately the same amount of short-term gain.

Adjustments to Unlisted Put or Call Option Price— Dividends, Rights, Etc.

Where the option price of an Unlisted Put or Call is to be adjusted because of any dividends, etc., the time the option is exercised may be an important consideration. For example, where an extraordinary, fully taxable dividend has been declared, the exercise of the Call after the ex-dividend date would reduce the acquisition price to the investor with a possible greater capital gain upon subsequent disposition. The dividend in this instance would be taxable to the previous holder of the stock, not the investor. Similarly, an investor should exercise a Put prior to the ex-dividend date in order to produce a greater long-term capital gain (assuming the stock was held for more than one year prior to the acquisition of the Put so as to avoid the short sales rules). If the Put is exercised after the ex-dividend date, the investor receives dividend income with a corresponding downward adjustment in the selling price of the stock resulting in reduced long-term capital gain. (See discussion of Puts and Calls on pages 91 to 103.)

> *Example:* T acquires a 30-day Unlisted Call on December 1, 1977 for $200 to buy 100 shares of XYZ stock at $30 (the current market price). XYZ stock will go ex-dividend an extraordinary fully taxable dividend of $5 per share on December 15, 1977. On December 14, 1977 XYZ stock is selling at $36 per share. If T exercises the Call prior to December 15, 1977, his basis in XYZ stock will be $32 per share ($30 purchase price plus $2 per share paid for the

Call). The market value of XYZ stock, assuming no further fluctuation in price, will drop to $31 per share after the stock goes ex-dividend the $5 dividend distribution. Then T will be taxed on the $5 per share dividend distribution and have a potential capital loss of $1 per share (basis of $32 less market value of $31). However, if T waited until December 15, 1977 to exercise the Call, the exercise price would be adjusted downward to $25 because of the dividend distribution. Thus T would be holding XYZ stock having a fair market value of $31 per share with a basis of $27 per share ($25 purchase price plus $2 per share paid for the Call). T would now have a potential $4 capital gain and no dividend income.

Use of an Unlisted Call and a Short Sale

Investors expecting a sharp and substantial, but temporary, rise in the market value of a security should consider buying a one year, ten-day Call on the stock and, when the expected rise occurs, selling the stock short. The investor thereby safeguards the amount of profit as of the desired moment of time and also retains the possibility of realizing such profit in the form of long-term capital gains. The cost of the Call, coupled with commissions and various other expenses, makes this method attractive only if a substantial but unstable rise in the market is expected. The Call is considered a capital asset in the hands of the investor, and, if sold after one year holding period at a gain, will result in a long-term capital gain.

Example: Let us assume that the investor on August 1, 1977 purchases for $5 per share ($500) a one-year, ten-day Unlisted Call on 100 shares of Z Corporation's stock at $20 per share. One month later, when the market value of Z stock has reached $30, the investor wants to insure his net economic gain of $5 per share ($30 market value of the stock less the cost of $20 and the cost of the Call of $5 per share). However, the investor would like to maximize the after-tax effect of the $5 gain by converting as much of the gain as possible into long-term capital gain. He therefore sells short 100 shares of Z stock at $30 per share. The short sale rules would not apply to any gain on the Call in this situation because a Call is not a security for this purpose. The longer capital gain holding period requirement (nine months for 1977 and one year for subsequent years) will adversely affect this type of transaction since the cost of the Call increases as the Call period is increased. Also note in the example below that greater economic gain can be realized if the stock substantially decreases in value after the short sale, but this is offset by the recognition of short-term gain in lieu of long-term gains.

Action on August 2, 1978 by the investor, with resulting tax effects, will depend upon the market value of the Z stock and may be summarized by the following chart (commissions and expenses of sale have been disregarded):

Market Price of Stock on August 2	Short-Term Gain (Loss) Per Share on Covering Short Sale	Long-Term Gain on Sale of Call (or Loss on Expiration)— Per Share	Net Economic Gain Per Share
$40	($10) short-term loss	$15 long-term gain	$ 5
30	None	5 long-term gain	5
27	3 short-term gain	2 long-term gain	5
15	15 short-term gain	(5) long-term loss (if Call expires)	10

LIMIT LOSS IN VOLATILE STOCK AND RETAIN POTENTIALITY OF LONG-TERM GAIN

The simultaneous purchase of an Unlisted Put and the underlying stock under certain circumstances (described on page 87) will prevent the Put from being treated as a short sale. This exception to the short sale rules allows the investor to limit any loss in the transaction to the cost of a Put, without sacrificing the possibility of long-term gain in the event the stock increases in value. The practical use of this transaction is limited to volatile securities which may have a substantial swing in market value in either direction.

Acquisition of an Unlisted Put Simultaneously with the Purchase of Stock

> *Example:* On May 1, 1977 T purchases 100 shares of ABC stock at $70 per share and at the same time buys a one-year, ten-day Unlisted Put on ABC stock at $70 for $1,000 ($10 per share). If the market value of the stock should fall to $30 per share, T could sell the stock for $70 by exercising the Put.

Thus T's loss is limited to the cost of the Put, $1,000. (It would appear that T could sell the Put for $4,000, recognizing a gain of $3,000, which should be given long-term capital gains treatment, provided the Put was held for more than one year. The stock could be sold immediately prior to meeting the one-year holding period requirement, resulting in $4,000 short-term capital loss. See page 87 for further discussion of this alternative.)

Should the stock rise substantially, for example, to $100 per share, T could sell his position, recognizing gain of $2,000 (cost of unexercised Put must be added to basis of stock) which would be given long-term gain treatment if the stock was held for more than one year. If T had sold the "worthless" Put prior to the one-year holding period, there is a possibility that the $1,000 paid for the Put would result in a short-term loss and that the long-term gain on the subsequent sale of the stock would be correspondingly increased.

Thus, T has limited any loss on the transaction to $1,000, the cost of the Put, and still has potential economic gain (long-term capital gain after one year) if there is a rise in the price of ABC stock.

OBTAIN LONG-TERM GAIN ON SALE OF APPRECIATED "WHEN-ISSUED" CONTRACTS

An investor who has held "when issued" stock for more than one year should consider, where practical, the private sale of the "when issued" stock (technically the sale of a contract to buy stock when and if issued) prior to settlement date, in lieu of the receipt of the new stock and the immediate sale thereof, or selling the "when issued" stock through a Stock Exchange. Gain realized on the private sale will be long-term while the sale of the new stock received, or of the "when issued" stock through a Stock Exchange, will cause the gain to be short-term (see discussion on page 104). This is similar to the sale of a Call held for more than one year as compared to the exercise thereof and selling the stock. (See page 94.)

> *Example:* T bought 100 shares of ABC stock "when issued" on November 1, 1977 at $30 per share. The "when issued" stock is scheduled to "go regular" on

December 1, 1978. Assume that on November 2, 1978, ABC "when issued" is selling for $50 per share. If T sells the "when issued" through the Stock Exchange, which is the usual transaction, the $2,000 gain will be considered to be recognized on the settlement date, December 15, 1978, as a short-term gain, even though the "when issued" stock had been held for more than one year. If T waits until December 15, 1978 to receive the "regular" stock of ABC, and then sells the stock at $50 on the next day, his $2,000 gain will still be short-term. T should sell the *"when issued"* contract on November 2, 1978, in a private sale in which case the $2,000 gain recognized will be treated as long-term.

With respect to "when issued" stock sold short (technically entering into a contract to sell stock for a fixed price when and if issued), the investor should sell or assign the contract-right rather than close out the short position. However, in this instance, it is questionable whether long-term gain will result even though the contract was held for more than one year. (See page 104.)

PROTECT GAIN ON EXERCISE OF A STOCK OPTION

A corporate executive or employee must not dispose of stock received upon exercise of a qualified stock option plan until the stock has been held for three years to qualify for long-term capital gain treatment [9] (Under a restricted stock plan created before 1964 the stock must be held for at least two years from the time of the grant of the option and six months after receipt of the stock).[10] The possibility of loss during the required holding period after exercise may be eliminated by purchasing an Unlisted Put concurrently with the exercise of the option.[11] However, the cost of a Put for the required three-year holding period for qualified stock options would generally be so high as to preclude this method of protecting the gain.

---

[9] Code: 422(a). Favorable treatment applies generally to options issued pursuant to plans in existence on May 20, 1976.

[10] Code: 424

[11] Rev. Rul. 59-242, C.B. 1959-2, 125

Another possible way of locking in the profit on stock acquired under a qualified or restricted stock option plan and still meet the requisite holding period, is to sell short a comparable number of shares of the stock ("short against the box"—see page 2). For determining the time gain or loss on the short sale is recognized, the stock is not deemed sold until the short sale is closed. Thus, under this rule a disqualifying disposition should not take place until the closing of the short sale. However, the Treasury has ruled that a short sale is considered a disposition of the stock for purposes of the three-year holding period requirement.[12] Another disadvantage to the use of a short sale is that the underlying stock must be held for more than one year before a short sale is made in 1978, so as to avoid the short sale rule denying long-term gain treatment (see page 84). If shares of another corporation in the same industry has had a similar price movement, the executive may consider hedging his investment by selling short the other stock. However, additional funds required for margin purposes may cause this hedge to also be impractical.

Because of the detrimental tax effects of exercising a qualified stock option (tax preference income and reduction of personal service income), and because of the interest costs during the three-year holding period, many executives should consider selling their stock prematurely in the same year of exercise, thus, removing the tax preference and realize personal service income subject to a maximum tax of 50 percent. A premature disposition also entitles the employer corporation to an ordinary deduction to the extent of the ordinary income reported by the executive, thereby presenting an opportunity for the executive to be awarded through a cash bonus for the tax benefits derived by the employer corporation from the premature disposition. The short swing rules should be considered. (See page 139.)

Officers, directors and 10 percent or more shareholders of listed corporations and other corporations required to file periodic reports with the SEC are apparently forbidden by the Securities Exchange Act of 1934 [13] to sell short the stock of their corporation or to go "short against the box" for more than a limited period.

---

[12] Rev. Rul. 73-92, C.B. 1973-1, 208   [13] Section 16(c)

CREATE LARGER CAPITAL GAINS—SALE OF EX-DIVIDEND STOCK "FOR CASH"

Assuming no other market fluctuations, the price of stock that goes ex-dividend is generally reduced by the amount of the dividend. The investor should sell the stock before, not after, the ex-dividend date, in order to produce greater capital gain by the amount of the dividend payment. Where the stock is sold after the ex-dividend date, but prior to the record date, the sale should be made "for cash." (See page 7.) The dividend under these circumstances belongs to the purchaser. However, the selling price of the stock is increased by the amount of the dividend and will thus result in greater capital gains to the seller.

ACCELERATE INCOME

Sometimes an investor may have sustained business or capital losses or may have incurred investment expenses or other deductions, such as medical expenses or casualty losses, which exceed his projected income for the year. Under the tax rules many of these excess expenses cannot be carried to other years and a failure to generate additional income will see these losses expire without tax benefit. Income can be generated by entering into a commodity straddle and selling the profit position in the earlier year. However, a capital loss is created in the later year rather than an ordinary loss. A similar use of a Treasury bill futures straddle may create an ordinary deduction in the later year (see Page 109). Other possible action is a sale of bond coupons (see Page 119) or of future dividends. See page 121 for general discussion of assignment of income.

AVOID WASH SALE RULES

In order to deduct a loss on securities for tax purposes and still maintain the same long position, a method frequently used in the past in order to avoid the wash sale rules, was the simultaneous purchase and short sale of the same security, and 31 days thereafter, the covering of the short position with the original shares held. The expected results were a recognition of the loss, and maintenance of the same long position with the lower basis. The Treasury has issued regulations [14] which, if upheld by the courts,

Short Sale— "Short Against the Box"

---

[14] Reg. 1.1091-1 (g)

43

would prevent this method of obtaining a deduction for the loss. (See page 83.) However, a variation of this short sale transaction might still be used effectively to accomplish the same objective of deducting the loss and maintaining the same long position. (See page 77 for discussion of wash sale rules.)

Other Methods

Investors sometimes avoid the wash sale provisions by replacing securities sold with securities in another corporation in the same industry. Another method frequently utilized is "doubling up" or buying an equivalent amount of the same issue, holding both lots for 31 days and then selling the original holding and recognizing the loss. This latter method has the disadvantage of tying up and risking additional capital. Of course the investor could sell the loss securities, wait 31 days and repurchase them. However, he is now without any economic interest in the securities for the 31-day period. A sale of the loss securities in January may result in greater proceeds than a sale in December if the securities are expected to drop further in value, because of tax-loss selling at the end of the year, and then recover. Tax factors alone should not affect economic decisions.

Sale of "In the Money" Puts

The wash sales provisions, disallowing a loss deduction, is triggered when within the 30 day period the taxpayer has acquired, or has entered into a contract or option to acquire, substantially identical property. The sale of the stock at a loss with a simultaneous sale of an "in the money" Put, where effective economic interest in the movement of the price of the stock (up to a certain point) remains with the investor, should not come within the technical requirements of the wash sales rules so as to disallow the loss deduction.

> *Example:* T owned 100 shares of X stock with a basis of $50 per share for more than one year. The current market value of X stock is $20 per share. T wishes to recognize a $3,000 long-term capital loss deduction without giving up his economic interest in the stock. Simultaneous with a sale of X stock for $20 per share, T could write a Put, with an expiration date of more than 30 days and with a strike price of $30. T will receive approximately $1,000 for the sale of this "in the money" Put. As long as X stock is selling at a price below $30, T will be assured

that the stock will be sold to him at $30 near the expiration date of the Put. T's tax basis will be the $30 per share paid less the $10 per share premium received on the sale of the Put, or a net of $20 per share. The 30 day acquisition period rule under the wash sales provisions will not have been violated. The sale of the "in the money" Put, (whether Listed or Unlisted) should not be considered as the acquisition of an option or absolute right to acquire the stock. If X stock should rise in value above $30 per share during the period of the outstanding Put, T's economic interest will disappear. He will not receive back the stock because the worthless Put will be allowed to expire unexercised, resulting in a short-term gain of $1,000. Therefore, T should make sure that the intrinsic value of the Put (the amount of dollars that the Put is "in the money"), is of sufficient size to take into account the possibility of a reasonable sudden rise in the value of the stock during the Put period.

Unlisted "in the money" Puts might also be used with securities (including tax-free municipals) to accomplish the above stated objective.

AVAILABLE TAX ELECTIONS

Allocation of Basis to Stock Rights Received

Where the fair market value of stock rights received is less than 15 percent of the value of stock, no allocation of the basis of such stock to the rights is made unless the investor so elects. If the investor intends to sell only the rights, or to exercise the rights with a view toward selling the newly acquired stock within one year, or before selling the old shares, an election to allocate the basis should be made in order to reduce the amount of gain recognized on the sale of the rights or the new shares. An election should also be made if the investor intends to sell both his old and newly acquired shares in order to maximize the long-term gains on the old shares and reduce the amount of short-term gains on the new shares. If the old shares are sold at a loss, an election should be made so as to reduce the amount of long-term losses. Where the investor intends to retain the stock acquired on exercise of the rights, there may be an advantage in not making the election if such action results in creating widely different bases which permit selective gain or loss on later sales. Where stock dividends are received, part of the basis of the old stock *must always* be allocated to the stock dividends. (See page 64 for discussion of the method of making the allocation to either dividend stock or rights.)

> *Example:* T owns 100 shares of X stock with a basis of $100 per share. He receives 100 rights to purchase more shares. The market value of the stock, on the first day traded ex-rights, is $180 per share and the rights are then worth $20 per right (less than 15 percent of $180). If T sells the rights at $20 each and makes no election, he will recognize $2,000 of gain (long-term or short-term depending upon the length of time the 100 shares of X stock were held). However, T may elect to allocate a portion of the basis of the $100 per share of X stock to the rights. Thus $10 ($100 times $20/$200) of basis would be allocated to each right. The gain that is recognized on the sale of such rights will thus be reduced to $1,000.

Obligations Issued at a Discount

An investor may elect in any taxable year to include in income annually the increase in the redemption value of certain noninterest bearing obligations issued at a discount, such as Series "E" savings bonds. Otherwise the entire discount element will generally result in ordinary income treatment in the year of redemption. The election is binding and applies to all such obligations owned and later acquired. All increases in value occurring in years preceding the election must be included in taxable income in the year of election. Investors, such as minors or retired persons with little or no taxable income, may find this election to be most advantageous.

Recognition of gain on the increased value of certain U.S. Government obligations not previously recognized as income in the years earned may be further deferred by exchanging them for other similar obligations. (See page 119.)

> *Example:* W purchased a $100 Series "E" savings bond for $75 in June, 1975. In 1977, she elects to include the increased annual redemption value in her income. At the end of 1977, between 2½ and 3 years have passed since the issuance date so W will recognize approximately $9.50 of interest income, which represents the full increment in value from date of purchase to the end of the year in which the election is made. (The amount of the increment depends upon the date of issuance of the savings bond and may be affected by an increase in rates

of return on such bonds.) Without such election, W would recognize $25 of interest income upon redemption of the bond at initial maturity. She could, based upon past precedents, continue holding such bond without recognizing income as Congress has not permitted any U.S. savings bonds issued since 1941 to finally mature. W could exchange the Series "E" bond for certain Series "H" bonds (which pay current interest) without being required to recognize any interest income represented in the increased value of the Series "E" bond and not previously reported as income. The interest represented by the increment in value would have to be reported when the Series "H" bonds were redeemed.

Amortization of Bond Premiums

Taxpayers in all tax brackets generally will find it advantageous to elect to amortize premiums paid upon the acquisition of taxable bonds. The allowable deduction for amortization operates to decrease ordinary income and to reduce the basis of the securities. The alternative is the maintenance of basis and a consequent capital loss or reduction of capital gain upon redemption or sale. (See page 112 for method of computation and restrictions.)

> *Example:* T purchases on January 21, 1977 a $5,000 10% ABC bond due January 2, 1987 for $5,500. T elects to amortize the premium of $500 over the 10-year term of the bond, thus obtaining annually a $50 ordinary deduction. Upon redemption in 1987 for $5,000, T will recognize neither gain nor loss, since the basis will have been reduced to $5,000. However, without such election, T would sustain a $500 long-term capital loss upon redemption ($5,500 cost less redemption amount of $5,000). Thus the election gives T annual deductions against ordinary income and may prevent capital loss upon subsequent sale or redemption of the bond.

UNDESIRABILITY OF LONG-TERM GAIN IN CERTAIN SITUATIONS

Normally an investor would prefer to have recognized gains on securities treated as long-term and losses treated as short-term. If an investor had large capital losses in the year, it is immaterial whether he realizes long-term or short-term capital gains, since the losses will offset any capital gain on a $1 to $1 basis. Therefore, an investor need not risk his potential gain by retaining the security until long-term gains can be obtained. Similarly, if an investor has only short-term gains or long-term gains, it is immaterial whether the losses are long-term or short-term because either type of loss can be fully offset against the capital gains. In this situation an investor should realize his long-term losses and save his short-term losses, if any, for use in future years. However, if the capital losses exceed the capital gains, it is preferable to have short-term losses which can be offset against ordinary income on a $1 to $1 basis, whereas $2 of long-term losses are required to reduce $1 of ordinary income. In a case where an investor has recognized short-term gains and long-term losses there is no benefit from realizing the long-term gains in that year. The long-term losses will merely offset the long-term gains, leaving short-term gains subject to tax at regular rates. Where possible the long-term gains should be deferred until the subsequent year, possibly by means of a short sale. (See page 83.) Realization of long-term capital gains, in lieu of short-term gains, is not advantageous where an investor has excess personal deductions, e.g., medical expense, charitable contributions, investment expenses, which cannot be carried to other years and the capital gains are less than the excess deductions. If the capital gains exceeds the excess deductions then it may be more advantageous to recognize long-term capital gains.

> *Example:* T has excess deductions of $10,000. His XYZ stock, which he has held for several years, has unrealized appreciation of approximately $10,000. He also owns ABC stock on which he has unrealized short-term gains of approximately $10,000. In this situation it would be preferable to sell the ABC stock since the ordinary deductions would offset the short-term gain. The long-term gain on the XYZ stock could be taken in a subsequent year. There would be no benefit in selling the XYZ stock in the loss year since the $6,000 capital gain deduction would be wasted because it cannot be carried over to another year. However, if the unrealized gain on the XYZ stock were $25,000, then the full $25,000 of long-term gain would not be subjected to tax because it would be offset by the $15,000 capital gain deduction and the $10,000 of excess ordinary deductions.

STOCK TRANSFER TAXES

Investors should be aware that the State transfer tax paid on the sale of stock is properly deducted as a tax and not merely as a sales expense in computing gain or loss in the transaction. This results in larger capital gains or smaller capital losses and an ordinary deduction. Although the tax savings may be small in amount, the amount may become significant where there have been many trades resulting in long-term gains. Treating the State transfer taxes as deductions will also produce extra tax deductions where the investor has net capital losses in excess of the $3,000 maximum deduction available after 1977. However, the deduction would be lost if the investor uses the standard deduction.

> *Example:* T had 200 separate transactions in various stocks selling above $20 (each transaction in 100 share lots) resulting in a net long-term capital gain of $20,000, computed by deducting New York State transfer taxes from the proceeds of sale. Approximately $1,000 of such transfer taxes would be paid and would be allowed as an ordinary tax deduction. Thus $21,000 will be given long-term capital gain treatment. If T had used the standard deduction, the $1,000 transfer tax would be wasted despite the fact that the capital gains have been increased from $20,000 to $21,000. It is questionable whether in this type of situation T could choose to reduce the capital gains by the transfer tax. If T had instead incurred a net loss of $20,000 computed in the same manner, only $3,000 would be allowed as a deduction against ordinary income. However, T should also claim a $1,000 ordinary deduction. The remaining loss of $13,000 ($20,000 less $1,000 transfer tax less $6,000 under the rule requiring $6,000 of long-term losses to offset $3,000 of ordinary income) will be available as a capital loss carry-over into future years.

INTEREST ON MARGIN ACCOUNTS

Interest charged on a stock brokerage margin account is deductible by a cash-basis taxpayer in the year in which credits such as dividends, cash deposits, or proceeds from sale of securities are made to the account sufficient to absorb the interest charge.[15] Therefore, a payment should be made into the margin account towards the end of December in order to assure the deduction of interest charges of that month and prior months where there have been no recent credits to the account of adequate amounts. This may be accomplished by mailing a check before December 31, although received by the broker in January, indicating the payment is for the unpaid interest. Prior to the 1976 TRA additional deductions could be created by prepaying the next year's interest on the margin accounts.[16] This is no longer permissible. (See page 125.) It should be noted that interest expense incurred on the purchase of taxable securities on margin may be partially disallowed if an investor owns or purchases tax-exempt securities for cash or through another account. Where an investor has also purchased a home, automobile, or other large personal expenditure, it is preferable for tax purposes to incur a liability for the personal expenditure rather than on the purchase of taxable securities. There would not be any disallowance of interest expense in the latter situation. Also note that the interest expense deduction may be subject to limitations, or may constitute a tax preference where certain deductions, including interest expense, exceeds 60 percent of adjusted gross income. (See page 140.) In the latter situation, it may be more beneficial to defer the interest expense to a subsequent year.

PREPAYMENT OF STATE INCOME TAXES

Where large capital gains are subject to State income tax, it may be advisable to prepay the State income tax in order to obtain the current deduction of such taxes. Otherwise, the deduction of the State income tax on the Federal income tax return for the following year may produce a much smaller benefit.

CONTRIBUTION OF APPRECIATED SECURITIES

Contributions after 1969 to public charities and certain private foundations of appreciated long-term securities will result in a contribution deduction (subject to a 30 percent limitation with the excess carried forward for 5 years) equal to the fair market value

---

[15] Rev. Rul. 70-221, C.B. 1970-1, 33   [16] Rev. Rul. 68-643, C.B. 1968-2, 76

of the property at the time of the gift. The appreciation in value escapes taxation. An election may be made to apply the 50 percent limitation rather than the 30 percent limitation to the contribution, but only 60 percent of the appreciation would be deductible. If a contribution is made to a private foundation, other than to an operating foundation or one which passes through all of its contributions to a qualified charity within $2\frac{1}{2}$ months of the following year, only 60 percent of the appreciation is deductible (subject to a 20 percent limitation).[17] Taxpayers who normally make charitable donations each year should still consider giving appreciated securities or sell securities to the charity at a discount in lieu of giving cash. The cash can be used to purchase the same or similar stock and thereby obtain a high tax basis for the stock. Donations of short-term securities should be avoided since no charitable deduction will be allowed for the appreciation. Depreciated securities should also not be donated but sold to establish a tax loss. The taxpayer would then donate the proceeds if there are no appreciated long-term securities which could be contributed.

> *Example:* T normally makes $1,000 of charitable contributions each year. T has owned for more than one year 100 shares of ABC stock with a fair market value of $10 per share, which cost him $1 per share. T should contribute these securities to a qualified charity. In this way, $900 of appreciation would escape tax. (See below for "bargain sales" of appreciated securities.)

Prior to 1979, taxpayers in the top tax brackets could have realized a greater profit by contributing shares with a low tax basis to charity rather than selling the shares and keeping the after tax proceeds. This would not be true for post-1978 taxable years, except perhaps for investors who reside in states which impose a large tax on capital gains, because the maximum tax rate on long-term capital gains has been reduced to 28 percent.

> *Example:* T, who is in the 70% tax bracket, owns 100 shares with a market value of $50,000 and a basis of $100. A sale before November, 1978 would result in net proceeds of approximately $32,500, assum-

---

[17] Code: 170(b)(1)(d) and (e), as amended by Section 402(b) of the 1978 RA, increasing the charitable deduction from 50 percent to 60 percent.

ing an aggregate capital gains tax and minimum tax of 35 percent. By donating the shares to charity, T would receive a charitable deduction which would increase his after tax income by $35,000. Thus, a gift to charity enabled T to realize an additional profit of $2,500. In addition, the charity of his choice received property worth $50,000. With the new maximum tax on capital gains of 28 percent, P would realize net proceeds of $36,000 on a sale, or $1,000 more than a contribution to charity. Thus, if T intends to benefit the charity by $50,000, he could do so at a very low cost. Any intended gift to charity should be with appreciated long-term stock that would otherwise have been sold, rather than cash, in order that the gain escape tax. This is true irrespective of the tax bracket of the taxpayer.

BARGAIN SALES OF APPRECIATED SECURITIES TO CHARITIES

A sale of appreciated securities to a qualified charity at their tax basis will also result in a contribution deduction (subject to percentage limitations) equal to the amount of appreciation. However, sales after December 19, 1969 are subject to tax. The amount of gain is determined by subtracting from the sales price a portion of the donor's basis, in the ratio of the sales price to the market value of the security.[18] Despite being partially taxable, a bargain sale of the security may result in greater after-tax dollars than an outright contribution of the security or a sale of the security followed by a cash contribution. Note that the effect of the bargain sales provision is to place the taxpayer in the same position as a sale of shares equal in value to the tax basis and a charitable contribution of the remaining shares. Use of the latter method, however, would result in additional transfer tax, additional sales commission (especially if there is an odd lot sale) and a possibly reduced sales price if there is a small market for this amount of shares.

> *Example:* T owns 100 shares of XYZ stock, purchased in 1968 at $40 per share. On February 1, 1978, this stock is selling at $100 per share. T, who is in the 50 percent bracket, wishes to close out his position and make a charitable contribution of $6,000. A sale would produce a $6,000 long-term gain and a

---

[18] Code: 1011(b); Reg. 1.1011-2

tax of $1,200. His after-tax proceeds will be $8,800 ($10,000 selling amount less $1,200 in taxes). After donating $6,000 to charity and thereby reducing his tax by $3,000, he will retain $5,800 after taxes. However, if T sells the 100 shares to a qualified charity for his cost of $4,000, he would be entitled to a $6,000 charitable deduction which would reduce his income taxes by $3,000. A $500 tax would be paid on the bargain sale (20 percent of $4,000 sales price less allocated basis of $1,600). Thus, T's after-tax proceeds would be $6,500 ($4,000 selling amount plus $2,500 net savings of income taxes), or $700 more than if the security was first sold and $6,000 of cash was donated to charity.

CAPITAL GAIN OR NONTAXABLE DIVIDENDS, AND TAX-EXEMPT INTEREST

A high-bracket investor should measure the income yield on invested capital in terms of after-tax dollars earned. Consideration should be given to investments offering tax sheltered yields such as securities in certain public utilities,[19] natural resources corporations, and trusts where part of the yield is considered a return of capital.

The investor should also compare his after-tax yield on savings bond interest, industrial bond interest and other income with interest income from tax-exempt state or municipal bonds.

The tax factors are recognized in the securities market in that variations in values do exist because of different tax treatment. For example, a U.S. Government obligation selling at a discount will sell at a price which produces a lower pre-tax yield than a U.S. Government obligation selling at par. This occurs because the discount will be treated as capital gain upon subsequent retirement.

TRANSFER OF APPRECIATED SECURITIES TO RELATIVES

High bracket taxpayers may effectively avoid the income tax on sales of appreciated securities by transferring them, at cost, to

---

[19] These tax-free dividends will disappear in many instances after June 30, 1972. Code: 312(m)

relatives, such as children, in lower tax brackets. The relatives, in turn, could sell the securities at the market value, recognizing (and paying tax on) the full appreciation. If the donor is of advanced age or there is no intent to sell the security in the immediate future, a step-up in basis could be obtained if the donor dies owning the shares. (See page 65). A gift of the securities could result in gift tax liability if the amount of the gift exceeded available exemptions and credits. The basis of the securities may be increased by the payment of gift taxes.[20]

> *Example:* T owns 100 shares of ABC stock purchased November 1, 1977 at $10 per share. On December 15, 1977 this stock is selling at $30 per share. If T, who is in the 50 percent bracket, sells such securities for full value, he will recognize $2,000 of short-term capital gain and pay a tax of $1,000. However, T could sell the 100 shares to his son for $1,000 and make a gift of the balance of the value. If there were no other gifts to his son during the year, there would be no gift tax on this transfer. Assuming the son is in the 19 percent tax bracket, he would pay only $380 of income taxes on the $2,000 short-term capital gain recognized by him upon the sale of the stock, as compared to $1,000 of tax that would have been paid by the father.

If the relative sells the securities as soon as he receives them, the Treasury may attempt to impute the gain to the high-bracket taxpayer, on the theory that the relative acted as his agent in making the sale. Therefore, it is helpful to be able to show that the relative acted as a free agent in his own behalf. This is usually easier to show in the case of an adult relative, and more difficult if the transfer is made to a minor for whom the high-braket taxpayer is guardian.

TRANSFER OF INCOME FROM SECURITIES TO RELATIVES

A high-bracket investor who is currently providing for the needs of an elderly or indigent relative or is saving for the future needs of the younger members of the family should consider setting up ten-year support trust.[21] A taxpayer in the 50 percent tax bracket

---

[20] Code: 1015 (d) [21] Code: 673 (a)

must earn $4,000 in order to give his needy relative $2,000. By placing securities in trust for at least a 10-year period with the income distributed annually, the trust income would be taxed to the trust beneficiary and not to the grantor. As a result of the beneficiary's increased personal exemption, increased standard deduction (if the beneficiary is not a dependent of the grantor or another person), and $100 dividends received deduction, at least $3,400 could be received by the beneficiary free of tax. If the beneficiary is a dependent of the grantor or another person, and, therefore, cannot utilize the standard deduction, then the amount of tax-free dividend and other income would be at least $1,100. Any additional income will be taxed at the lowest tax brackets. Alternatively, an investor can avoid the expense of creating a support trust by taking advantage of the current high yields on tax-exempt bonds. By receiving the tax-free interest and giving it to his dependent, the investor can also claim a deduction for the dependent's personal exemption and any medical expenses paid in his behalf.

> *Example:* T, who is in the 50 percent bracket, gives his elderly mother $2,000 annually from his dividends and interest. To obtain the $2,000 after-tax amount, T must receive $4,000 of income and pay a $2,000 tax on the income. If T sets up a trust for his mother for a period of ten years or his mother's life, whichever is shorter, with the trust principal reverting to T at the end of the period, the income would be taxed to T's mother and not to T. For years after 1978, T's mother is entitled to a personal exemption of $2,000 (over age 65), a standard deduction of $2,300 and a dividend exclusion of $100. Instead of paying a $2,000 tax on the income, T's mother would pay no tax and would have $4,000 for her personal needs. However, approximately 45 percent of the value of the securities placed in trust would be subject to gift tax.

GOVERNMENT OBLIGATIONS ACCEPTABLE IN PAYMENT OF FEDERAL ESTATE TAXES

Certain U.S. treasury bonds selling at a discount are redeemable at face value in payment of Federal estate taxes. The carryover basis rules would have eliminated most of the tax saving opportunities for large estates because an income tax would have been imposed on the redemption of the U.S. Treasury bonds. However, with the postponement of the carryover basis rules, substantial savings in estate tax can be accomplished by the purchase of these bonds by an individual with a short life expectancy. (See page 121.)

DEATH BED SALES

The 1976 TRA provisions had eliminated certain estate tax savings devices, such as making death bed gifts of security or other property or purchasing "flower bonds" to pay Federal estate taxes. A deferral of the effective date of the basis carryover provision again makes it fashionable to hold appreciated property until death in order that the decedent's estate or beneficiaries will obtain a higher tax basis for the securities (see page 65). However, there are other tax benefits that can be obtained from death bed tax planning for securities.

An investor with depreciated securities should sell the securities before death to offset any capital gains for the year and to obtain the maximum deduction for capital losses that can be offset against ordinary income ($3,000 for years after 1977). At death, the lower fair market value will become the tax basis of the securities in the hands of the decedent's estate or beneficiaries. (See page 65.)

A conflict as to whether to sell before death or to get a basis step-up at death but risk a decrease in the value of the stock can be resolved by "selling short against the box." (See page 2.) A short sale will preserve the economic value of the stock and the gain on sale can be averted by delaying the closing of the short position until after the death of the investor. (See page 89.) An alternative to a short sale would be an installment sale. Gain on the sale could be deferred until the sales proceeds are received by electing the installment method. (See page 8.) Thus, if the decedent's estate or beneficiaries would be in a lower tax bracket, the deferral of the sales proceeds would result in the estate or beneficiaries paying less taxes on the gains. In addition, they would be entitled to a deduction for the estate taxes payable on the unpaid installment gain.

If an investor has capital losses or net operating losses from his business, he could realize capital gains before death to take advantage of these losses since they will expire at death even if he files a joint return with his surviving spouse. Of course, with the postponement of the basis carryover rules, his estate or beneficiaries would also escape tax on the appreciation since the new tax basis of the inherited stock generally would be its fair market value at time of death. Again, the decedent may wish to sell the appreciated securities because he anticipates a downturn in the market. As an alternative the surviving spouse can make use of the capital losses or net operating losses by selling her appreciated securities. These sales can occur before or after the death of the investor, provided they take place in the year of death and a joint return is filed for such year.

PRINCIPLES OF TAXATION
OF SECURITIES TRANSACTIONS

INTRODUCTION

A general coverage of the income tax provisions applicable to transactions by an individual investor, on a cash basis, in publicly traded securities is given in this section. Also included is a summary of the tax provisions affecting other types of investors. The existence of complex tax rules necessitates a limited discussion of some types of securities transactions. A review of the 1976 Tax Reform Act (1976 TRA) and the Revenue Act of 1978 (1978 RA) provisions that may have a direct or indirect effect on securities transactions also is included in this section. Note that for the sake of simplicity, a more than one-year holding period for long-term capital gains is used in the text and examples although the holding period for long-term capital gains is more than six months for years prior to 1977 and more than nine months for 1977.

Time of Reporting Income or Deductions A cash basis investor generally will include dividend income, interest income and gains on the sale of securities in his gross income in the year in which cash or other property is received.[22] Thus, dividend income is not included in income at the time the dividend is declared or when the dividend check is issued by the distributing corporation, but when the check is received by the

---

[22] Reg. 1.446-1(c)(1)

shareholder even if received in the following year.[23] A dividend of property other than cash, however, is valued at the date of distribution although received at a later date.[24] Gain on the sale of securities is also taxed in the year the sale proceeds are received and not the day the transaction was entered into ("regular way" sales). In the case of stock sold on an exchange, the settlement date and not the trade date is controlling.[25] Ordinarily, the settlement date will be the fifth business day following the trade date. Interest expense, transfer taxes and other deductible investment expenses are also deductible when paid rather than at the time incurred. Losses on the sale of securities, however, are deductible on the trade date even though delivery and receipt of the proceeds occurs in the subsequent year.[26] A cash basis investor may cause the gain to be recognized in the year of the trade by making the sale "for cash." However, gain or loss on the closing of a short sale of securities, or on the closing of a short (or written) listed option will be reflected in the year the settlement date occurs because the controlling event is the delivery of the securities.[27]

All securities held by investors except short-term U.S. or other Government obligations issued at a discount, without interest, are considered capital assets.[28] Capital gains or losses are determined by taking the difference between the sales price or proceeds received and the tax basis of the security (usually cost of the security). Sales, exchanges or redemptions of publicly traded securities will, in general, result in capital gains or losses which are divided into two basic classifications: long-term and short-term. For taxable years beginning before 1977, a sale or exchange of a security would generally result in a long-term gain or loss if the security was owned for more than six months. A shorter holding period (see page 69) would result in a short-term gain or loss.[29] Under the transitional rules of the 1976 TRA, the holding period for long-term capital gains is extended to more than nine months for taxable years beginning in 1977 and is further increased to more

General Rules for Capital Gains and Losses

---

[23] Reg. 1.451-2(b); Rev. Rul. 68-126, C.B. 1968-1, 194
[24] Reg. 1.301-1(b)
[25] Harden F. Taylor, 43 B.T.A. 563 (1941); Rev. Rul. 72-381, C.B. 1972-2, 233
[26] Rev. Rul. 70-344, C.B. 1970-2, 50
[27] Code: 1233 and 1234

[28] Code: 1221(5). A sale of securities by a *trader*, who is not a dealer in the securities, results in capital gain or loss. *H.M. Adnee*, 41 TC 40 (1963); *L.J. Kabernat*, T.C. Memo. 1972-1320, *Van Suetendael*, 152 F. 2d 654, (CA-2, 1946).
[29] Code: 1222

than one year for taxable years beginning after 1977.[30] In the case of binding contracts entered into in one year where part or all of the proceeds of sale are received in a subsequent year, the holding period rule for the year the gain or loss on the sale is realized rather than the year the gain or loss is recognized or reported for tax purposes is to be used in determining whether the amounts received are subject to long-term or short-term capital gain treatment.[31] Thus, if a security is sold at a profit at the end of 1976 but the settlement date is in 1977, the 1976 (more than six months) holding period rule governs. Similarly, if securities are sold in 1976 and the seller elects to report the gain under the installment method pursuant to Section 453, the six-month holding period rule for 1976 is to be applied in determining whether the seller will recognize long-term or short-term gain on receipt of the installment payments in subsequent years. Note, however, that if the sale is not consummated until a subsequent year, as in the case of a short sale,[32] the controlling year for determination of the applicable holding period rules will be the year the transaction is closed and gain or loss is realized, and not when the parties entered into an executory contract of sale. The six-month holding period rule remains in effect for future transactions in any commodity subject to the rules of a board of trade or commodity exchange.[33] However, the longer holding period rules will apply to a sale of a commodity, as distinguished from a commodity futures contract, even if the commodity is used to close the futures transaction. For example, if in July 1977 an investor buys a spot commodity contract, and sells a futures contract which requires delivery after the seventh month, the closing of the futures contract with the spot commodity will be subject to the general rules in effect for 1978. A sale of a Call, Put or other security option will also fall under the general rules even if the option is with respect to a security that is sold over a commodity exchange. See page 105 for a full discussion of rules applicable to commodities.

All long-term transactions are netted to produce a net long-term gain or loss. Short-term transactions are similarly netted. Net long-term gains are reduced by net short-term losses (referred to in the Internal Revenue Code as "net capital gain"); net short-term gains are reduced by net long-term losses.[34]

---

[30] 1976 TRA: 1402(a)
[31] 1976 TRA: 1402(c)
[32] Reg. 1.1233-1(a)(1)

[33] Code: 1222; IR 1787 (3/30/77)
[34] Code: 1222

A deduction of 60 percent is allowed against net capital gains (net long-term gains less net short-term losses) realized on sales or exchanges after October 31, 1978 or proceeds from prior sales received after such dates.[35] Note that the capital gain deduction will no longer be treated as a tax preference subject to a minimum tax of 15 percent for taxable years beginning after 1978.[36] Instead, the capital gain deduction will be included in a new alternative minimum tax with a maximum rate of 25 percent.[37] (See page 141). However, the capital gain deduction for net capital gains recognized for the short period after October 31, 1978 will still be subject to the 15 percent minimum tax. Because of the lower effective tax rates on net capital gains, the alternative capital gains tax of 25 percent on the first $50,000 of net capital gains has been eliminated for taxable years beginning after 1978.[38] For high bracket investors with personal service income taxed at a maximum rate of 50 percent, net capital gains recognized after October 31, 1978 will no longer increase the effective maximum rate on the personal service income.[39] The sum total of these amendments is that the maximum rates on net capital gains will be reduced from approximately 50 percent to 28 percent. Most investors will not be affected by the repeal of the alternative tax since they do not realize more than $50,000 of net capital gains in one taxable year (except perhaps from lump sum distribution from a qualified employee benefit plan and a special ten-year income averaging can be used in this case), nor will they be affected by the alternative maximum tax. They will benefit, however, from the increased 60 percent capital gains deduction which when coupled with the reduced general tax rates results in a much lower tax rate on net capital gains. Investors who previously paid an effective rate of 25 percent will find that their rate may be reduced below 20 percent, and in some cases may be less than 6 percent. Net short-term gains in excess of net-long term losses are taxed as ordinary income. Income averaging may also be used for both types of capital gains if it will result in a lesser tax. (See page 142.)

[35] Code: 1202, as amended by 1978 RA: 402(a) ; Rev. Rul. 79-22. A 50 percent deduction is allowed for pre-November 1, 1978 net capital gains. Under the transitional rule for 1978, a 60 percent deduction is allowed on the lesser of the net capital gains for the short period after October 31, 1978 or the net capital gains for the entire year. Any additional net capital gains for the taxable year would be entitled to a 50 percent deduction.

[36] Code: 57(a) (9) (A) as amended by 402(b)

[37] Code: 55 as amended by 1978 RA: 402(b)

[38] Code: 1201(b) (2), as amended by 1978 RA: 401(a)

[39] Code: 1348(b) (2) (B), as amended by 1978 RA: 441

Where there is a net capital loss sustained in or carried to taxable years beginning after 1977, the amount of the loss allowed as a deduction against ordinary income is limited to $3,000 or the taxable income for the year, whichever is smaller.[40] Previously, the deductible amount was $1,000 for taxable years beginning before 1977, increased to $2,000 for years beginning in 1977.[41] Married persons filing separately can deduct only one-half of the otherwise deductible amount against their ordinary income.[42] Thus, for the year 1978, each spouse could apply up to $1,500 of his or her net capital loss against ordinary income. Short-term capital losses, including short-term loss carryovers, are to be first deducted against ordinary income up to the applicable amount for the year.[43] If there are no short-term losses or they total less than the applicable amount, then long-term losses may be deducted to the extent of the difference. For years beginning after 1969, only 50 percent of an investor's net-long term losses may be deducted from ordinary income subject to the above-mentioned applicable limitation.[44] The ratio of $2 of long-term capital loss against $1 of ordinary income has not been changed despite the fact that the net capital gains deduction has been increased to 60 percent for post-October 31, 1978 transactions. Thus, for 1978, long term losses of $6,000 must be used to obtain a $3,000 ordinary deduction. Any amount in excess of $6,000 may be carried over to succeeding years, but the non-deductible half of the $6,000 will be lost.[45] Long-term losses arising in years before 1970 continue to be deductible in full subject to the applicable limitation.[46] Pre-1970 long-term capital losses are first deductible against ordinary income before long-term capital losses incurred in the current year.[47] For example, if in the above example there were remaining long-term capital loss carryovers from pre-1970 taxable years of $8,000 and the investor incurred a $4,000 long-term capital loss in 1978, $6,000 of the pre-1970 long-term losses are applied against ordinary income in 1978 and the remaining $2,000 pre-1970 long-term loss plus the $4,000 long-term loss from 1978 are carried to 1979, with the pre-1970 long-term loss having priority over any long-term losses incurred in 1979 in reducing ordinary income for 1979. Note also that long-

---

[40] Code: 1211(b)(2) as amended by 1976 TRA: 1401(a) and (b)

[41] Code: 1211(b)

[42] Spouses filing separately for pre-1977 taxable years could each carryover and apply $1,000 of their pre-1970 capital losses against their ordinary income. Post-1969 capital losses are limited to the $500 maximum in effect for those years. Rev. Rul. 72-105, C.B. 1972-1, 228.

[43] Code: 1211(b)(1)

[44] Code: 1211(b)(1)(c)(ii)

[45] Code: 1212(b)(2)(B)

[46] Code: 1212(b)(3)

[47] Rev. Rul. 71-195, C.B. 1971-1, 225

term losses may be deducted in full against short-term gains. For this purpose long-term losses incurred in the current year would be applied first against short-term gains.

Capital loss carryovers are now allowed for an unlimited period, but the losses retain their original character. Capital losses sustained after 1963 are carried over separately as long-term or short-term losses, depending upon the nature of the losses in the year sustained and are combined with the losses of the same category for the succeeding year as if they had been incurred in such succeeding year.[48]

Treasury regulations provide specific rules for allocating capital carryovers between husband and wife where a joint return is filed in one year and separate returns are filed in another year.[49] Generally spouses are treated as separate taxpayers who are permitted to combine their capital gains and losses as though they were one individual by filing a joint return. Thus, capital losses from separate returns may be carried over and applied in a joint return. Excess capital losses may be carried from one joint return to another. Where separate returns are filed in a subsequent year, however, the long-term and short-term capital losses are each separately apportioned between the spouses in accordance with the amounts of such losses each contributed. For example, if the husband had $2,000 of long-term gains and $2,000 of short-term losses, and the wife had $2,000 of long-term losses and $3,000 of short-term losses, the husband would be entitled to forty percent ($2,000 short-term losses over $5,000 total short-term losses) of the short-term capital loss carryover even though on a separate return basis he would have no excess capital loss for the year. Upon the death of a spouse the decedent's share of the unused capital losses in the final joint return cannot be carried over by the surviving spouse, nor by the decedent's estate or beneficiaries.[50]

BASIS OF SECURITIES

The investor has the burden of proof in establishing the basis of a security sold. The Treasury may be able to impose a lesser or zero basis in the event the burden is not met.[51] Thus the importance of accurate record-keeping is self evident.

In General

---

[48] Code: 1212(b)(1), before amendment
[49] Reg. 1.1212-1(c)
[50] Rev. Rul. 74-175, C.B. 1974-1, 52

[51] *Eder*, 9 TCM 98 (1950); Biggs, T. C. Memo. 1968-240; see infra for special rule when property is acquired by gift.

Purchase   The tax basis of securities acquired by purchase is ordinarily the cost of acquisition, including the commissions paid. Interest equalization tax, if applicable for purchases before July 1, 1974 (see page 139), is added to the basis of the security. Securities received in exchange for other securities in a corporate reorganization or other nontaxable exchange will generally take the same basis as the securities exchanged. On the other hand, if the exchange is taxable, the fair market value at such time becomes the basis of the securities.[52] Reference to published Capital Changes services will ordinarily provide the information necessary to establish basis for any publicly-held security received in an exchange or distribution.

Taxable Distribution   The basis of securities received by the investor in a taxable corporate distribution is the fair market value at such time.[53]

Stock Dividends and Stock Rights   The general rule is that a portion of the basis of the "old" stock is allocated to a nontaxable stock dividend (or right).[54] The allocation is based upon fair market values of the stock or rights received in relation to the fair market value of the "old" stock at the time of distribution. Where a stock distribution is taxable, e.g., is treated as a cash dividend [55] or consists of stock of another corporation, the basis of the stock will be the same as the amount of the dividend income to the shareholder. Reference to published Capital Changes services will provide the necessary percentage of allocation.

Where the fair market value of rights at the time of distribution is less than 15 percent of the value of the stock, no allocation is made and the basis of the rights is zero, unless the investor elects to make the allocation under the general rule.[56] The allocation *must always* be made where stock dividends are received regardless of the market value of the properties.

Gift   Securities acquired by gift (after 1920) have a basis for purposes of determining gain equal to the donor's basis. For purpose of determining loss, the fair market value of the property at the time of the gift, if less than the donor's basis, is used.[57] Thus it is possible under certain circumstances that neither gain nor loss will

---

[52] Rev. Rul. 55-757, C.B. 1955-2, 557
[53] Code: 301 (d) ; Reg. 1.301-1 (h)
[54] Code: 307; Reg. 1.307-1

[55] Code: 305
[56] Code: 307 (b) ; Reg. 1.307-2
[57] Code: 1015 (a) ; Reg. 1.1015-1

be recognized. Where it is impossible to determine the basis of the donor, the fair market value at the time the donor acquired the property will be the basis to the donor for purposes of determining the donee's basis.[58]

The donee's basis for securities received as a gift before 1977, as determined under the above rules, is increased by the amount of gift tax paid with respect to the gift, but not above the fair market value at the time of the gift.[59] With regard to gifts received after 1976, the donee's basis is increased only by the portion of the gift tax paid on the net appreciation in the value of the gift, i.e., the excess of fair market value at time of gift over donor's basis.[60] For example, if a gift tax of $2,000 was paid on a gift of $100,000, of which the net appreciation was $10,000, the donor's basis would be increased by $200 (10 percent of $2,000). Where the donor died before 1977 and the securities received as a gift are included in the donor's taxable estate, the basis of the securities to the donee is generally the value used for estate tax purposes.[61] (See page 69 for effect on holding period.) However, the carryover basis rules apply to deaths after 1976. (See the following paragraph). In this event the donee will retain the holding period of the donor.[62]

For deaths occurring before 1980, securities received by inheritance take a basis equal to the value used for estate tax purposes (fair market value at date of death or if alternate value is elected, the value six months after death [63] or at date of earlier disposition).[64] An heir, however, ordinarily is not bound by the valuation used for estate taxes and is allowed to use a correct valuation unless he is prevented from using another valuation because of his involvement in the estate tax valuation.[65]

Inheritance

A complex carry-over method for determining the basis of securities received by inheritance has been deferred and will apply only to deaths occurring after 1979.[66] In general, the adjusted basis of the deceased owner immediately before death will be used, in-

---

58 Reg. 1.1015-1(a)(3)
59 Code: 1015(d)
60 Code: Section 1015(d)(6) as amended by 1976 TRA: 2005(c)
61 Reg. 1.1014-6
62 Code: 1223(2)
63 A one year period is used for decedents dying before 1971.
64 Code: 1014 as amended by 1978 RA: 515

65 *Hess, Jr.*, 537 F.2d 457 (Ct. Cls. 1976); *Ford*, 276 F.2d 17 (Ct. Cls. 1960); Rev. Rul. 54-97, C.B. 1954-1, 113
66 Code: 1023 as amended by 1978 RA: 515. A senate amendment permitting an election of carryover basis for deaths after 1976 but before the effective date of the 1978 RA was not adopted.

creased by any federal and state estate or inheritance taxes paid by the estate or heir on the net appreciation in the value of the securities, i.e., the excess of fair market value at date of death over decedent's basis. In determining decedent's basis, any increase in basis resulting from the "fresh start rule" discussed below, must be taken into account. Thus, if an estate tax of $5,000 is paid on a security which is valued at $10,000 at time of death but with an original tax basis of $1,000 which is increased to $8,000 under the "fresh start rule", the basis would be further increased by $1,000 (20 percent of $5,000).

If all of the eligible carryover basis property of the decedent had a fair market value at death of at least $60,000 and an adjusted tax basis of less than $60,000 after making the above described adjustments, including the "fresh start" adjustments, then the basis of all of the eligible property will be increased on a pro-rata basis, based on respective net appreciation in value, to $60,000. However, the adjustments for death taxes and the $60,000 minimum tax basis cannot increase the basis of any property above its fair market value at death.

In the event that the heir cannot determine the basis of the inherited securities (the executors or administrators of the estate of the deceased are required to furnish this information) then the fair market value at the approximate time the decedent acquired the security or his holding period began, may be used.

A special "fresh start rule" was enacted in order to avoid any income tax on appreciation that incurred before 1977.[67] This rule applies only to inherited securities and not to post-1976 sales made by the decedent prior to death. In determining gain realized on the sale of marketable bonds or securities held by the decedent at the end of 1976 or which had a carryover basis, the fair market value on December 31, 1976 should be used. Marketable bonds and securities include any security regularly traded over a national, local, or foreign stock exchange or over-the-counter market for which quotations can be regularly obtained. This should include bonds, stock, warrants or stock options which are regularly traded, but not options or other convertible securities which are

---

[67] Code: 1023(h)

convertible into a marketable security but which do not themselves have quoted values.[68] Non-marketable securities received after 1976 in a tax-free exchange for marketable securities held at December 31, 1976 qualify, but not marketable securities received after 1976 in exchange for non-marketable securities held at the end of 1976. As indicated previously, the basis carryover rules including the fresh start rule, are not applicable to deaths prior to 1980.

While the committee report [69] indicates otherwise, the regulations provide that the adjusted tax basis can exceed the value of the security reported on the estate tax return.[70] Note that the decedent's adjusted basis is used where a loss was realized on the transaction or there was no appreciation on December 31, 1976. It is possible to have neither gain nor loss recognized on marketable securities held by a decedent on December 31, 1976 and sold after his death. For example, stock acquired for $10, has a fair market value at December 31, 1976 of $100. At death, after 1979, the fair market value of the stock is $95, and the stock is sold by the estate for $95. No gain or loss would be recognized on the transaction. Assume that the stock was worth $95 at death, but upon subsequent sale, $101 is realized. Under these circumstances, the adjusted basis is $95 and a $6 gain is recognized. No loss would be recognized unless the stock is sold below $10.

In determining gain on a non-marketable security owned by a decedent on December 31, 1976 the adjusted tax basis of the security is increased by the appreciation attributed to the period before 1977. This is computed by allocating a portion of the appreciation at the time of death, based on the holding period before and after December 31, 1976. For example, if the decedent acquired the non-marketable security on January 1, 1975 at a cost of $2,000 and died on December 31, 1980 when its fair market value was $5,000, the basis is increased by $1,000 (2/6 of $3,000 appreciation).

In order to apply this fresh start rule with respect to non-marketable securities and other property, the adjusted basis and

---

[68] Conference Committee Report, H. Rep. No. 94-1515, 94th Cong., 2d. Sess. at pg. 612 (1976) The normal method of valuation for estate and gift tax purposes is to be used in determining the value of such securities on December 31, 1976, i.e., mean between high and low for listed securities, mean between bid and ask for over-the-counter securities, etc.

[69] Conference Committee Report, H. Rep. No. 94-1515, 94th Cong., 2d. Sess. at pg. 612 (1976)

[70] Reg. 7.1023 (h)-1

approximate date of acquisition by the decedent must be known. The executor or heirs may not have such information, making the adjustment to basis difficult or impossible.

It is expected that changes will be made to the basis carryover rules before they become effective in 1980.

Qualified Employee Pension Plans   The Basis of employer securities or other securities distributed by qualified employee plans, including pension plans, thrift plans and employee stock ownership plans (ESOP), will include both the aggregate amount of the employee contributions plus any gain realized on the distribution.[71] The entire net unrealized appreciation on employer securities is not taxable if a lump sum distribution in termination of the employee's interest is made to the employee; otherwise only the net unrealized appreciation attributable to the employer securities is excluded from tax.[72] Thus, by electing a lump sum distribution an employee can escape tax on the entire net unrealized appreciation on employer securities. Any gain realized on a lump sum distribution is either subject to long-term capital gains treatment with respect to pre-1974 employer contributions or may be subject to a special 10-year averaging convention.[73] A capital gains tax will be paid on the excluded net appreciation only when the employer securities are ultimately sold.

Miscellaneous   The basis of securities may require adjustment due to distributions treated as a return of capital,[74] tax-free spin-off of a subsidiary corporation,[75] partial liquidation of a corporation,[76] redemption through use of related corporations,[77] deemed dividend distribution,[78] undistributed capital gains of an investment company,[79] bond premium which the investor has elected (or has been required) to amortize[80] (see page 112), annual adjustment for original issue discount on bonds issued after May 27, 1969[81] (see page 114) and stock rights and stock dividends received.[82] Refer-

---

[71] Reg. 1.402(a)-1(b)
[72] Code: 402(e)(4)(J)
[73] Code: 402(a)(2), 402(e)(4)(E)
[74] Code: 301(c); 1016(a)(4)
[75] Code: 355
[76] Code: 346

[77] Code: 304
[78] Code: 305(b)
[79] Code: 852(b)(3)(D)(iii)
[80] Code: 1016(a)(5)
[81] Code: 1232(a)(3)(E)
[82] Code: 307

ence to published Capital Changes services will generally provide the necessary information regarding distributions, etc.

HOLDING PERIOD

The determination of the holding period of securities is important in order to ascertain the nature of the gain or loss on their sale. With respect to pre-1977 sales, securities held for more than six months would generally result in long-term capital gain or loss, while a sale of securities held for not more than six months would generally cause the gain or loss to be treated as short-term. The holding period for long-term capital gain treatment has been increased to more than nine months for 1977 sales and to more than one year for post-1977 sales. The investor has the burden of proving the length of time he has held the securities.[83]

Introduction

Acquisition by Purchase: The period of ownership is measured in terms of whole months rather than in days. This period begins on the day after acquisition and ends on the day of sale. Stock acquired on the last day of a calendar month must have been held at least until the first day of the seventh succeeding month, in order to be held "long-term" for pre-1977 sales.[84] For example, stock acquired on April 30 and sold on October 31 is not considered as being held for more than six months. However, stock acquired February 27 and sold August 28 is considered as being held for more than six months.

Measurement of Holding Period

The *trade dates* are the controlling dates. Therefore, dates of delivery of stock or securities and payment (which may be delayed by holidays) generally have no effect.[85]

In an exception to the usual rule, the holding period of stock received upon the exercise of stock rights includes the day of exercise (acquisition of the stock).[86] The holding period of stock acquired through the exercise of a call begins the day after the acquisition of the stock.[87]

---

[83] *Taylor*, 76 F. 2d 904 (CA-2, 1935)
[84] Cf. Rev. Rul. 66-7, 1966-1, C.B., 188
[85] I.T. 3705, C.B. 1945, 174; Rev. Rul. 66-97, C.B. 1966-1, 190; Rev. Rul. 70-

344, C.B. 1970-2, 50
[86] Code: 1223(6); Reg. 1.1223-1(f); Rev. Rul. 56-572, C.B. 1956-2, 182
[87] *Weir*, 10 T.C. 996 (1948)

The date payment is received (ordinarily the settlement date) on securities sold on a stock exchange will determine the year in which gain is to be recognized.[88] However, with the probable exception of a deferred delivery under New York Stock Exchange rule 64(3) (see page 19), the holding period terminates on the trade date for purposes of determining whether the transaction is long-term or short-term.[89] The trade date determines the year in which a loss on a sale of a security is deductible.[90] (See page 7 for further details.) In the case of a short sale, gain or loss is recognized in the year the transaction is closed. (See page 84.)

The holding period of securities acquired as the result of the acquisition of a "when issued" contract begins the day after the securities are actually acquired, not when the contract is purchased.[91] Where buy and sell contracts of securities trading on a "when issued" basis are not sold or exchanged prior to their maturity, but are retained until settlement date, the sale and purchase of the underlying securities take place on the settlement date, resulting in short-term gain or loss.[92]

Stock scrip represents a fractional share of stock and its holding period will depend upon the manner in which it is acquired. Scrip received in payment of accrued interest or a taxable dividend is income in the year received and its holding period begins when the scrip is acquired.[93] The issuance of scrip in lieu of fractional shares as part of a stock dividend is nontaxable until sold and it will tack on to its holding period the holding period of the underlying stock.[94] Similarly, the holding period of scrip received in other nontaxable transactions, including reorganizations and reverse stock splits whereby a shareholder exchanges his shares for a smaller number of shares, will include the holding period of the shares surrendered in the tax-free exchange. Where a shareholder purchases additional scrip in order to receive a full share of stock, the basis of the additional scrip purchased will be the purchase price of the scrip and its holding period will commence the day after purchase.[95]

---

[88] Rev. Rul. 72-381, C.B. 1972-2, 233
[89] Rev. Rul. 70-598, C.B. 1970-2, 168
[90] G.C.M. 21503, C.B. 1939-2, 205
[91] I.T. 3721, C.B. 1945, 164
[92] *Shanis*, 19 T.C. 641 (1953), aff'd per curiam 213 F. 2d 151 (CA-3, 1954)

[93] *Andrews*, 46 BTA (1942) (ACQ.); *Patterson* v *Anderson*, 20 F. Supp. 799 (D.ct. N.Y., 1937)
[94] Rev. Rul. 69-202, C.B. 1969-1, 95
[95] See footnote 97, infra

Losses from worthless securities are deemed to have occurred on the last day of taxable year of worthlessness.[96]

Tax-Free Exchange: Stock acquired through the conversion of the issuing corporation's convertible bond will have a holding period beginning with the holding period of the bond. Where a cash payment is necessary in the exchange, the portion of each share of stock represented by such cash payment will receive a new holding period.[97]

Illustration: Assume a convertible bond was purchased on February 1, 1978 for $100. On October 1, 1978, when the underlying stock is worth $200, the bond is converted into 1 share of stock with the payment of an additional $50. The conversion is tax-free, but the share of stock will have a split-holding period for purposes of determining long-term or short-term gain or loss. That part of the share attributable to the bond will have a basis of $100 and a holding period relating back to the purchase of the bond whereas the portion of the share attributable to cash paid on conversion will have a basis of $50 and a holding period beginning with the day following the conversion date. However, since the stock on the conversion date had a value of $200, $150 or $3/4$ of such value is attributable to the bond and $50 or $1/4$ is attributable to the $50 cash payment. On any subsequent disposition of the share, $3/4$ of the sales price will be attributable to the bond portion for purposes of determining the amount and the character (short- or long-term) of the gain or loss. The remaining portion will be attributed to the $50 payment as shown by the following table:

1. Sales price	200	300	160	150	60
2. Amount attributable to bond	150	225	120	112.50	45
3. Gain or loss attributable to bond	50	125	20	12.50	(55)
4. Amount attributable to $50 payment	50	75	40	37.50	15
5. Gain or loss attributable to $50 payment	0	25	(10)	(12.50)	(35)

---

[96] Code: 165(g)

[97] Rev. Rul. 62-140, C.B. 1962-2, 181

In general, where the investor exchanges securities in a tax-free transaction, and the basis of the securities received is determined in whole or in part with reference to the basis of the securities given up, there will be a tacking on of the holding period of the property exchanged.[98]

Taxable Exchanges: Securities received in a taxable exchange, taxable reorganization, corporate distribution or liquidation, generally will have a new tax basis equal to its fair market value and, thus, will also receive a new holding period. The new holding period will commence from the time of the exchange, similar to a purchase of securities. However, in the case of a one month liquidation under Section 333, the holding period of any securities received in the liquidation will include the holding period of the investor's stock in the liquidated corporation.[99]

Gifts: A donee receiving securities as a gift may tack on to his holding period the holding period of the donor, provided that upon sale of the securities the donor's basis is required to be used, in whole or in part, in determining gain or loss on the transaction.[100] The donor's basis is always used where securities received as a gift after 1920 are sold at a gain, but if the securities are sold at a loss, the basis of the securities is the lower of the donor's basis or the fair market value at the time of the gift.[101] Where the fair market value is lower, the donee's holding period starts at the date of the gift without any tacking on of the donor's holding period.[102]

The Treasury has ruled that if stock is purchased and placed in a margin account in joint names, then there is no completed gift.[103] Under this questionable ruling, presumably all income is attributed to the donor. No gift occurs until the donee withdraws the stock or other funds from the account.

If a gift of security is made by a donor who died before 1977 and the value of the security is reported in the donor's estate tax return (value at date of death or alternate value) because the gift was

---

[98] Code: 1223(1)
[99] Code: 334(c)
[100] Code: 1223(2). The donor's holding period is used even if the donee is required to pay the gift taxes. *Turner,* 410 F. 2d 952 (CA-6, 1969)

[101] Code: 1015(a)
[102] I.T. 3453, C.B. 1941-1, 254 (declared obsolete by Rev. Rul. 69-43, C.B. 1969-1, 310)
[103] Rev. Rul. 69-148, C.B. 1969-1, 226

considered to have been made in contemplation of death [104] or the donor retained certain rights in the security,[105] the holding period of the security would start at the date of the gift. There would be no tacking on of the donor's holding period because the donor's basis was not used in determining the donee's basis.[106] With respect to post-1979 deaths however, since the basis carryover provisions [107] apply to gifts includible in the donor's estate tax return because made within three years of death or because of retention of certain rights, the donee will tack on the donor's holding period.[108] Note, to the extent the gifts are not includible in the donor's gross estate because of the $3,000 gift tax exclusion,[109] there would also be a tacking on of the donor's holding period under the regular gift rules.

Death: The holding period of securities inherited from a decedent who died before 1980 owning the securities relates back to the date of death. However, the securities are considered to have been held by the estate or heirs for the period required for long-term capital gain or loss treatment, even if held for less than one year, nine months or six months, as the case may be.[109a]

If the carryover basis provisions become effective in 1980, the holding period of inherited securities will be the same as the decedents. This is true even if the December 31, 1976 value is used as the basis. The automatic long-term capital gain or loss treatment for executives or heirs will be available after 1979.[109b]

The 1978 RA extended the effective date of the basis carryover provisions and, thus, indirectly continued the automatic long-term capital gain or loss treatment for executives or heirs for an additional three years. The new legislation extended the automatic capital gain treatment beyond 1979.

With respect to securities purchased by the estate or testamentary trust, the holding period starts from the date of such purchase. In general, the date of distribution to the beneficiary is not significant in determining the beneficiary's holding period.[110]

---

[104] Code: 2035
[105] Code: 2036-2038
[106] Rev. Rul. 59-86, C.B. 1959-1, 209
[107] Code: 1023 as amended by 1976 TRA: 2005(a)
[108] Code: 1223(2)
[109] Code: 2035 as amended by 1976 TRA: 2001(a)
[109a] Code: 1223(11)
[109b] Code: 1223(11) as amended by 1978 RA: 702(b)(5)
[110] *Brewster v. Gage,* 280 U.S. 327 (1930)

Wash Sales: (See page 77.)

Stock Rights and Nontaxable Stock Dividends: Stock rights and stock dividends received in a nontaxable distribution take the same holding period as the "old" stock.[111] Thus, when stock rights are sold, the holding period of the "old" stock is "tacked on" in determining the holding period of the rights. However, securities acquired through exercise of the rights will not take on a "tacked on" holding period. The holding period will start on the date of exercise.[112]

Short Sales: (See page 83.)

IDENTIFICATION OF SECURITIES

Importance of Identification

Where an investor holds various lots of securities acquired at different times or at different prices, and sells only a part of his holdings, the proper identification of which securities are sold has great significance in determining the tax effect of the sale. Because of differences in holding periods and bases, a sale may result in either short-term or long-term gain or loss, depending upon which securities are deemed sold. Adequate record-keeping on the part of the investor will enable him to control the type and amount of gain or loss to be recognized when a portion of a position is sold.

Rules of the Regulations

The Treasury has provided certain guidelines, consistent with court decisions, with respect to the identification of securities sold.[113]

Securities Held by Brokers, Banks, etc.: Where securities are held by a broker in a cash or margin account or by a bank or other custodian or agent, an adequate identification of the securities sold is made if the investor specifies to the broker or other agent at the time of the sale, the particular securities to be sold and written confirmation is received from the broker or other agent within a reasonable time thereafter.[114] The designated securities are treated as sold even though the broker, etc., delivers other securities to the

---

[111] Code: 1223(5); Rev. Rul. 72-71, C.B. 1972-1, 99.

[112] Code: 1223(6); Reg. 1.1223-1(f); Rev. Rul. 56-572, C.B. 1956-2, 182

[113] Reg. 1.1012-1(c)

[114] Reg. 1.1012-1(c)(3)(i)

transferee. Identification of the securities sold from the account should be by purchase date, cost or both.[115]

Securities Held by Investor: Where securities are held by the investor, the securities sold will be those represented by certificates actually delivered, even if the investor intended, or instructed the broker to sell securities from a different lot.[116] However, where a single certificate represents securities acquired at different times or at different prices, the investor will have made an adequate identification of the portion sold, if he specifies the particular lot to be sold by identifying the purchase date, cost or both, of the securities, and written confirmation thereof is received from the broker within a reasonable time thereafter.[117] If transfer of part of the securities represented by a single certificate is made directly to the purchaser and not to a broker, adequate identification is made where the investor maintains a written record of the particular securities which he intended to sell.[118]

First-in, First-out: Where the investor cannot "identify" the lots from which the securities are sold, he is required to apply the first-in, first-out ("FIFO") rule, so that the securities sold are deemed to be the earliest acquired. On the other hand, if delivery is made from lots held at a particular source, then the FIFO rule applies only to securities held at that source.[119] Thus, where the investor delivers stock from lots held by broker A and other lots are held by broker B, the FIFO rule will apply only to the lots held by broker A. The FIFO rule has also been applied to the transactions in "when issued" securities.[120]

For purposes of the FIFO rule, the earliest acquisition date has been interpreted to mean the earliest beginning date of a holding period for purposes of determining gain or loss.[121] Thus, although there is some conflict in this area, the acquisition date for securities received as a gift should be the first day of the holding period and not necessarily the date of gift.[122] Nontaxable stock dividends are

---

[115] Reg. 1.1012-1(c)(2)
[116] Reg. 1.1012-1(c)(2); *Davidson*, 305 U.S. 44 (1938)
[117] Rev. Rul. 61-97, CB 1961-1, 394; see also TIR No. 334, 8/17/61
[118] Reg. 1.1012-1(c)(3)(ii)
[119] Reg. 1.1012-1(c)(1)
[120] I.T. 3858, C.B. 1947-2, 71

[121] *W. A. Forretser*, 32 BTA 745 (1935); *Curtis*, 101 F. 2d 40 (CA-2, 1939); *Helvering v. Campbell*, 313 U.S. 15 (1941)
[122] *Richardson v. Smith*, DC, Conn. (1938), rev'd on other issues 102 F. 2d 697; contra *Hanes*, 1 TCM 634 (1943)

treated as having been acquired at the time of the original stock purchase. Stock acquired through the exercise of rights is deemed acquired when the rights were exercised. If a portion of such stock is sold and there is no specific identification, the stock deemed sold is that acquired through exercise of rights received from the earliest held stock (FIFO rule).[123]

Securities Held by Trust or Estate: Where the securities are held by the fiduciary of a trust or estate (and not by a broker or other custodian), adequate identification is made if the fiduciary specifies in writing in the trust's or estate's records at the time of disposition the particular security to be sold, transferred or distributed. A distributee must get written notification of the particular security distributed to him. The identified security is treated as sold, transferred or distributed even though other securities are in fact delivered.[124]

Regulated Investment Company Stock (Mutual Funds): The basis of regulated investment company stock generally is computed in the same manner as stock of a regular corporation. Additional shares acquired through reinvestment of dividends, including capital gain dividends, will have a tax basis equal to the amount of the dividend income taxed to the investor. If a regulated investment company elects to treat undistributed capital gains as having been distributed to its shareholders, the shareholders should increase the tax bases of their shares by 70 percent (72% for post-1978 capital gains) of the undistributed capital gains.[125] In determining the tax basis of shares sold, an investor may use FIFO or specific identification. However, if stock of a regulated investment company purchased or acquired at different prices are left with a custodian or agent appointed by the regulated investment company for that purpose, an investor may elect an average basis in lieu of the regular methods of identification.[126] Either the double-entry method (the shares are segregated into short-term and long-term capital gains stock) or single-category method (average cost of all shares in the account) may be elected.

---

[123] GCM 11743, C.B. XII-2, 31; *Keeler,* 86 F. 2d 265 (CA-8, 1936), cert. den. 300 U.S. 673

[124] Reg. 1.1012-1(c)(4)

[125] Code: 852(b)(3)(D)(iii)

[126] Reg. 1.1012-1(e)

Identification is possible where securities are exchanged in a tax-free reorganization. One arbitrary method of identification that has been accepted is the assigning of the lowest numbered new certificate to the earliest lot purchased.[127] In a partial liquidation, the shareholder may specifically identify the shares to be redeemed or exchanged for newly issued shares; identification is not negated because the designations were recorded incorrectly on the corporation's record.[128] In absence of identification, the FIFO rule will be applied in determining gain or loss of the cancelled shares and the basis of the newly issued or remaining shares.[129] The subsequently promulgated regulations relating to identification where a single certificate represents securities acquired at different times (see page 74) may also be applicable to these transactions.

Where adequate identification is not made and securities in the same corporation are received, the courts have generally held that the first-in, first-out method must be used.[130] However, where securities of another corporation are received in a tax-free reorganization and adequate identification is not made, the cost of the securities surrendered is averaged and allocated equally among the new securities received.[131]

WASH SALES

Where an investor sells stock or securities at a loss and within a 30-day period before or after such sale acquires substantially identical securities, the loss will be disallowed as a "wash sale."[132] It is immaterial whether the securities purchased or sold had been purchased on margin.[133] (For the definition of "substantially identical" property see the discussion on page 87 of the short sales rules, to which the term also applies.)

The entering into a contract or option to acquire substantially identical securities within the 61-day period will be treated as an

---

[127] *Ford*, 33 BTA 1229 (1936) (A)

[128] Rule 127 F. 2d 979 (CA-10, 1942)

[129] *Allington*, 31 BTA 421 (1934)

[130] *Kraus*, 88 F. 2d 616 (CA-2, 1937); cf. *Fuller*, 81 F. 2d 176 (CA-1, 1936); but cf. *Big Wolf Corp.*, 2 TC 751 1943(A)

[131] *Von Gunten*, 76 F. 2d 670 (1935); cf. *Bloch*, 148 F. 2d 452 and Rev. Rul. 55-355, C.B. 1955-1, 418

[132] Code: 1091(a). Note that an individual *trader* who qualifies as being in the business of buying and selling securities is exempt from the wash sale provisions, but a corporate investor is not excluded unless it is a *dealer* in securities. Reg. 1.1091-1(a).

[133] Rev. Rul. 71-316, C.B. 1971-2, 311

actual acquisition for purposes of the wash sale rules. Thus the purchase of a "Call" (Listed or Unlisted) will bring into play the wash sale rules. A purchase of a convertible preferred stock has also been ruled to be an acquisition of an option for wash sales purposes.[134] Apparently, the purchase of a convertible debenture would be accorded similar treatment. Only acquisitions by purchase or in a fully taxable exchange result in disallowance.[135] Therefore, receipt of securities as a gift or in a nontaxable exchange will not be considered an acquisition.

Employer stock received as a bonus under a work incentive plan, within 30 days from the sale of other bonus stock at a loss, is treated as an acquisition of stock for purposes of the wash sale rules.[136] Presumably a receipt of stock from a qualified employees' plan, e.g., pension plan, stock bonus plan, employee stock ownership plan (ESOP), will also be treated as an acquisition. See below for similar treatment of employee stock options.

The basis of the substantially identical securities acquired within the 61-day period will, in effect, be increased by the amount of the disallowed loss.[137] The holding period of the securities sold at a loss will be tacked on to the newly acquired position.[138] Thus, if the old securities were held for five months and the newly acquired securities were held for more than seven months, long-term gain or loss would be recognized on the sale of the new securities.

Stock Rights, Warrants and Options The Treasury has ruled that stock warrants come within the definition of "options" to acquire, which may cause the disallowance of a loss.[139] Thus, deduction of a loss on the sale of stock, where a warrant to buy the stock is purchased within the 61-day period, will be denied because the investor has acquired an option to buy the stock. However, it is unclear whether under Section 1091(d) a disallowed loss because of the purchase of a Call is added to the basis of the acquired Call. Similarly, with respect to the holding period of the stock sold at a loss it is also unclear as to whether under Section 1223(4) such holding period is added to the holding period of the option. (See page 99 for a complete discussion of the issues.)

---

[134] Rev. Rul. 77-201, I.R.B. 1977-23, 16
[135] Reg. 1.1091-1(f)
[136] Rev. Rul. 73-329, C.B. 1973-2, 302
[137] Code: 1091(d)
[138] Code: 1223(4)
[139] Rev. Rul. 56-406, C.B. 1956-2, 523

With respect to stock rights it is arguable that the receipt of a stock right on stock held, where a sale of the underlying stock occurs within 30 days of the receipt of the right, should not bring into play the wash sale provisions, provided the right is not exercised within the 30 day period, since the investor has not "entered into an option." However, the Treasury has ruled in a related situation, that where an employee is granted a stock option under a restricted or qualified stock option plan, for purposes of the wash sale rules, he will be deemed to have entered into an option to acquire stock on the date on which the option is granted to him.[140]

The sale of an option (stock right, warrant, etc.) and the subsequent purchase of a substantially identical security must be distinguished from a sale of a stock or security followed by the purchase of an option. The wash sales rule only applies to a loss realized on a sale of a stock or security. Section 1091 and its underlying regulations are silent as to whether a warrant or other type of option constitutes a stock or security. There are conflicting rules in other tax areas as to whether these options are a stock or security. A right to subscribe to a security is considered a security in the tax provisions affecting security dealers [141] and exchanges pursuant to SEC orders,[142] but not for purposes of corporate reorganizations.[143] The Treasury has impliedly ruled that a warrant is a security [144] and it may take the same view with respect to other types of options, e.g., Listed Puts and Calls. The sale of a Listed option at a loss with a subsequent repurchase within 30 days of the identical Listed option will cause the wash sales rules to apply only if a Listed option is deemed to be a "security" within Section 1091. (See below as to the "Substantially Identical" issue). The purchase of a Listed option "to close" at a loss with a subsequent resale within 30 days of the identical Listed option is not a wash sale because you generally need two purchases and one sale to come within Section 1091 and, under these circumstances, there are two sales and only one purchase.

The Treasury has resolved a dispute among the courts [145] as to whether a commodity future contract is a security for purposes of

---

[140] Rev. Rul. 56-452, C.B. 1956-2, 525
[141] Reg. 1.1236-1(c)
[142] Reg. 1.1083(f)
[143] Reg. 1.351-1(a)(ii) and 1.354-1(e)
[144] Rev. Rul. 56-406, C.B. 1956-2, 523

[145] *Trenton Cotton Oil*, 147 F. 2d 33 (CA-6, 1945); Corn Products Refining Co., 215 F. 2d 513 (CA-4, 1954), aff'g. 16 T.C. 395 (1951), aff'd. on other issues 350 U.S. 46 (1955)

the wash sales rules by ruling that the wash sales provisions do not apply to commodity futures transactions.[146] Losses on foreign currencies are also excluded from the wash sales provisions because foreign currencies are not securities for these purposes.[147]

A second consideration is whether the subsequently acquired stock or security is "substantially identical" to a stock right, warrant, call or other option. In general, the term has the same meaning as when used for purposes of short sales.[148] A Call has been ruled not to be substantially identical to the underlying stock for purposes of the short sale rule.[149] On the other hand, a loss on sale of a warrant was disallowed on grounds that its relative value and price changes were so similar to the later acquired stock as to make the warrant a fully convertible security and therefore substantially identical.[150] This might be the case where the stock is selling above the exercise price of the warrant so that fluctuations in the stock directly affect the market value of the warrant. The ruling did not consider other factors, such as a limited life and lack of dividend rights, in deciding that a warrant was substantially identical. Bonds issued by the same governmental agency have been ruled to be not substantially identical because of different dates of issue, dates of interest payments, maturity dates or interest rates,[151] and similar considerations should apply to warrants and other options. Stock rights more closely resemble calls than warrants because of the substantial difference between market price and option price and the shorter time available for exercise of the option. Generally, these different forms of options should not be considered substantially identical to the underlying stock or security, but as stated above, under certain conditions a warrant will be treated by the Treasury as substantially identical.

If Listed options are deemed to be a security for purposes of Section 1091, then the question exists as to when are Listed options substantially identical to each other. Listed options with different striking prices and/or different expiration dates should not be substantially identical to each other.[152] However, Listed options with the same striking price and expiration date trading on differ-

---

146 Rev. Rul. 71-568, C.B. 1971-2, 312
147 Rev. Rul. 74-218, C.B. 1974-1, 202
148 Reg. 1.1233-1(d)(1)
149 Rev. Rul. 58-384, C.B. 1958-2, 410
150 Rev. Rul. 56-406, C.B. 1956-2, 523

151 Fn. 186 *infra*.
152 See Page 110 dealing with commodity futures transactions and the "substantially identical" issue.

ent exchanges might be deemed to be substantially identical to each other.

Losses will not be disallowed where there is a bona fide sale of securities made to reduce the investor's holdings purchased in one lot, even though the sale is made within the 30 days after the securities were purchased and even though such transaction would literally come within the statutory provisions.[153] However, the wash sale rule was held to be applicable when separate lots were purchased on the first and fifteenth day of the same month, and the last purchase was sold at a loss on the twenty-ninth day of the same month.[154] This latter ruling is inconsistent with the concept that the wash sale rule should not apply to a transaction where the Taxpayer is merely reducing his holdings notwithstanding the acquisition in two separate lots.

Reduction of Holdings

Where there have been multiple purchases of identical securities at different prices and the wash sale provision applies to only some of the securities sold, matching of the sales and purchases are in the order of the date of the earliest acquisition.[155] Thus, if 100 shares are purchased on February 1 for $100 and 100 shares purchased on March 1 for $50, and the 200 shares are subsequently sold on December 1 for $10, followed by a repurchase on December 15 of 100 shares, the $90 loss on the first acquisition will be disallowed, but the $40 loss on the second acquisition is deductible.

Different Lots

The wash sale rules are not applicable where the stock is sold at a gain and immediately repurchased. Sales of different lots at the same time are treated separately in determining gain or loss on the shares of each lot. For example, if lot A is purchased at $20 a share and lot B at $50 a share, and all the shares are sold at $45 a share, the loss on the sale of the shares of lot B may be disallowed under the wash sales rules.[156] Prior to enactment of the provision for unlimited capital loss carryover,[157] investors would accelerate gain in order to wipe out any capital loss carryover that was about

Gain Recognized

---

153 Rev. Rul. 56-602, C.B. 1956-2, 527
154 Rev. Rul. 71-316, C.B. 1971-2, 311
155 Reg. 1.1091-1(c) ; Rev. Rul. 70-231;
   C.B. 1970-1, 171
156 Rev. Rul. 70-231, C.B. 1970-1, 171
157 Code: 1212(b)

to expire. Such action is now rarely advantageous except possibly to offset long-term losses against short-term gains.

Sales to Related Parties The wash sale provisions do not specifically deny a loss deduction where another member of the family or other related party purchases the same security within the 61-day period.[158] However, an attempt to circumvent these rules by having the investor's wife buy back securities sold by the investor at a loss has been frustrated by the Supreme Court under another section of the Internal Revenue Code,[159] on the ground that there was an indirect sale of the stock to the wife.[160] The wife had used her own funds, but the repurchase on the open market had occurred on the same day as the sale at substantially the same price.

Where the repurchase is at a different time and price so that there is not a "direct or indirect" sale between related parties, the loss should not be disallowed even though the repurchase by a related party is within the 61-day period.[161] If a wife is using her husband's funds and acting as his agent to repurchase the stock within the 61-day period, the transaction could be attacked as not being bona fide and the loss will probably be disallowed under the wash sale rules. Similarly, if there is an "understanding" that the securities will be repurchased the loss will be disallowed.[162]

Effect of Short Sales The regulations [163] treat a short sale as a true sale for purposes of the wash sale rules *if* on such date, the taxpayer owned (or had a contract or option to acquire) securities identical to those sold short *and* subsequently delivered them to close the short sale. When these conditions are not met, the short sale is deemed to occur when it is closed out by delivery of the securities. The regulations are intended to preclude the avoidance of the wash sale rules by use of the *Doyle* [164] plan ("short against the box"), which consisted of making a simultaneous short sale and purchase of the securities, waiting for just over 30 days, and then delivering the certificates representing the original holding to close out the short sale. As the regulations apply only in interpreting the wash sale rules, they do not

---

[158] *Norton*, 250 F. 2d 902 (CA-5, 1958)
[159] Predecessor of Code section 267; the loss would be allowed to the wife (transferee) only to the extent of the recognized gain upon subsequent sale.
[160] *J. P. McWilliams*, 331 U.S. 694 (1947)
[161] *Norton*, 250 F. 2d 902 (CA-5, 1958)
[162] *Mellon*, 36 BTA 977 (1936); E. E. Hassen, 63 T.C. 175 (1974)
[163] Reg. 1.1091-1(g) and 1.1233-1(a) (5)
[164] *Doyle*, 286 F. 2d 654 (CA-7, 1961)

change the rules applicable to short sales generally. Therefore, the technique of going short against the box to postpone the recognition of gain would not be affected. (See page 2.)

See page 43 for discussion of ways of avoiding the wash sale rules. According to the Treasury, a contract for deferred delivery (see page 19) will not be a means of circumventing the wash sale rules.[165]

Avoidance of Wash Sale Rules

SHORT SALES

A short sale of securities may be defined as a contract for the sale and delivery of securities the seller does not own or does not intend to make available for delivery on the sale. The securities are usually borrowed for delivery to the buyer. Such sale may be ultimately covered by the purchase of the securities in the market or by the delivery of secuirties already owned but not delivered to the buyer at the time of sale.[166]

Definition

The taxable event occurs only when the securities are delivered to close the short sale.[167] This rule is applicable whether gain or loss is realized on the sale.[168]

Taxable Event

In general, the holding period of the property delivered to close the short sale determines whether a long or short-term gain or loss results.[169] However, statutory rules have been established with respect to "substantially identical property" in order to prevent use of short sales to convert short-term gains into long-term gains or to create artificial long-term gains and short-term losses. "Property" for this purpose includes only stock and securities including those dealt in a "when issued" basis, and commodity futures which are capital assets in the hands of the taxpayer.[170] A purchase of a spot commodity contract and a sale of a commodity future ("cash and carry transaction") would not come within the short sale rules since only commodity futures and not the actual commodity are considered property for purposes of the short sale rules. However, the new holding period rules will apply if the commodity is used to cover the futures contract since the six month provision applies

Statutory Rules

---

165 Rev. Rul. 59-418, C.B. 1959-2, 184

166 *Provost,* 269 U.S. 443 (1926); Rev. Rul. 72-478, C.B. 1972-2, 288

167 Reg. 1.1233-1(a)

168 *Hendricks,* 51 TC 235 (1968)

169 Reg. 1.1233-1(a)(3)

170 Code: 1233(e)(2)(A)

only to commodity futures. (See page 69 for additional details on holding period.) The meaning of "substantially identical property" is discussed *infra*.

The rules may be summarized as follows:

Rule 1: If property substantially identical to that sold short has been held by the taxpayer (or his spouse)[171] on the date of the short sale for not more than one year (six months and nine months for taxable years beginning before 1977 and in 1977, respectively)[172] or is acquired by him after the short sale but before the closing thereof, then
   A. any *gain* on the closing of such short sale shall be considered as a short-term gain (even if property held for more than one year is used to close the short sale);[173]
   B. the *holding period* of such substantially identical property becomes "tainted" and is considered to begin on the date of the closing of the short sale, or on the date of a sale, gift or other disposition of the property, if earlier.[174] The "tainting" of the holding period will apply to only an equal quantity of substantially identical property in the chronological order of its acquisition. This rule does not apply to any excess over the quantity sold short.

Rule 2: If substantially identical property has been held by the taxpayer (or his spouse) for more than one year at the time the short sale was made, any *loss* on closing the short sale is considered a long-term loss even if the property delivered to close the short sale was held for not more than one year.[175]

Where the taxpayer holds both short-term and long-term positions in securities substantially identical to the securities sold short, all the above rules will be applicable. Accordingly, any gain on sale would be short-term and any loss would be long-term.

Illustration: Investor T purchases one share of X stock on February 1, 1978 for $10 and an additional share on April 1, 1978 for

---

[171] Code: 1233(e) (2) (C); Reg. 1.1233-1 (d) (3)
[172] 1976 TRA:1402(b) (1) (T)
[173] Code: 1233(b) (1); Reg. 1.1233-1(c) (2)
[174] Code: 1233(b) (2); Reg. 1.1233-1(c) (2)
[175] Code: 1233(d); Reg. 1.1233-1(c) (4), Note that if a security was held for less than one year at the time of the short sale but for more than one year at the time the short sale was closed, any loss realized on the sale would be long-term under the regular rules. Reg. 1.1233-1(a) (3)

$20. T sells short one share of X stock on March 1, 1979 at $30. On December 1, 1979, the X stock is selling at $40. If T then delivers the one share purchased February 1, 1978 in order to close out the short sale position, the $20 gain will be treated, by application of rule 1(a), as short-term since substantially identical property (one share of stock purchased April 1, 1978) had been held "short-term" on the date of the short sale. In addition, the holding period of the one share of X stock purchased on April 1, 1978 is "tainted" and is considered, by application of rule 1(b), to begin on December 1, 1979, the date of the closing of the short sale. However, if the April 1, 1978 position was used to close the short sale, the gain of $10 would be short-term under rule 1(a), but the holding period of the February 1, 1978 position would not be affected since such stock was held for more than one year at the time of the short sale. If T closed his short position by purchasing one share of X stock on December 1, 1979 at $40, the loss of $10 would be a long-term capital loss by application of rule 2 since substantially identical property had been held at the time of the short sale for more than one year. The holding period of the April 1, 1978 position would be "tainted" and would be considered by application of rule 1(b) to begin on December 1, 1979, the date the short sale was closed.

An open question would appear to be whether the holding period "taint" rolls over to other substantially identical stock if the "tainted" stock is sold. Thus, where the investor purchases 100 shares of X stock on March 1 and 100 shares of X stock on March 3 and sells short 100 shares of X stock on May 15, the holding period of only the 100 shares purchased March 1 will be "tainted." If the March 1 stock is sold, and the short position is left open, do the short sale rules result in the March 3 stock becoming "tainted"? No further affirmative act seems to have occurred so as to bring the short sale rules into operation once again.

Transitional Rules: 1976-1977-1978: The holding period of the long position at the time of the short sale will determine whether or not the short sale rules come into play. However, the normal holding period rules at the time of the closing of the short sale will determine whether the requisite holding period was met to have long-term treatment. For example, assume the stock was held for 10 months at the time of the short sale in December 1977. The holding period of the long position is not tainted and lost because the long position was held for more than 9 months and, accordingly, the short sale rules do not activate. Thus, the holding period of the long position continues to run. However, if the short position is closed in January 1978 by delivery of the long position, then held for 11 months, the required more than one year holding period in effect in 1978 is not met and any gain or loss would be short term. (See page 69 for further details on holding periods.)

Options to Sell: The acquisition of an option to sell stock at a fixed price (referred to as a "Put") is considered as a short sale for purposes of rule 1 above and the exercise or failure to exercise such option is considered as a closing of the short sale.[176] However, the acquisition of a Put is *not* considered a short sale for purposes of rule 2 above and the exercise or failure to exercise such option is *not* considered as a closing of the short sale.[177]

Note, that once the Put is acquired (other than on the same day— see below), the holding period of an equivalent amount of stock, which is held less than one year, is lost and will not start over again until the Put is disposed of. This is true even though the stock is sold later at a loss. Thus, if stock is purchased in 1978 for $21 per share and eleven months later a nine-month Put is purchased with a striking price of $20, a sale of the stock five months thereafter at $20 will produce a short-term capital loss because the eleven month holding period would be lost due to the purchase of the Put.

In addition, rule 1 is not applicable if a Put and the stock intended to be used in exercising the Put are acquired on the same day, provided the stock is actually so used if the Put is exercised. Where the option does not specifically identify the property intended to be used in exercising the option, the taxpayer's records must, within 15 days after the acquisition of the stock, contain such identifica-

---

176 Code: 1233(b); Reg. 1.1233-1(c)(3); Special Ruling, September 7, 1973, 74-9 CCH ¶6596. This private ruling originally indicated that the sale of the previously purchased Put would retroactively reinstate the original holding period of the long stock position. A subsequent private ruling, dated April 30, 1976, retracted the IRS's original erroneous interpretation of the short sale rules. Thus, the subsequent disposition of an acquired Put will merely start the commencement of a new holding period for the stock.

177 Code: 1233(d); Reg. 1.1233-1(c)(4)

tion. If the Put is not exercised, its cost is added to the basis of the stock with which it was identified.[178]

Where the market value of the stock has fallen so that an Unlisted Put has increased in value, the Put could be sold and, if held for more than one year, the gain will be long-term.[179] This should occur since the acquisition of the Put was not considered a short sale because of the exception discussed above. The stock could be sold prior to the long-term holding period in order to have the loss sustained treated as a short-term capital loss. (See example on page 39 and discussion on page 91.) However, repeated sales of Puts under similar circumstances could negate the taxpayer's "intention" to exercise the Put with the designated stock. Under such circumstances, it could then be argued that the exception would not apply in the case of any Puts the taxpayer acquired. If this argument prevailed and the stock appreciated in value, the holding period would be 'tainted" by Rule 1, since the acquisition of the Put would be considered as a short sale.

Note that the writing of a Put does not constitute a short sale and should not be confused with the acquisition of a Put. Consequently, if a Put is written at the time when the grantor held the underlying stock for less than the one year period for long-term gains, the writing of the Put will not affect the holding period of the underlying stock.[180]

The short sale rules apply only when the investor holds other securities substantially identical to the securities sold short. The solution to the perplexing problem of what this term means is far from clear. Treasury regulations indicate that the term is to be applied according to the facts and circumstances in each case and generally is to have the same meaning as when used in the "wash sale" provisions.[181] This discussion covers the meaning of the term applicable to both the wash sale and short sale rules. Based upon Treasury rulings and court decisions, certain guidelines have been established.

Substantially Identical Property

Stocks and securities of one corporation, although not ordinarily considered to be substantially identical to stocks and securities of

---

[178] Code: 1233(c); Reg. 1.1233-1(c)(3)   [180] Ibid
[179] Special Ruling, September 7, 1973,   [181] Reg. 1.1233-1(d)(1)
    74-9 CCH Para. 6596

a different corporation, may be so considered if the corporations are predecessor and successor in a reorganization where their securities are exchanged.[182]

Where two corporations have agreed to a merger, subject to approval by shareholders, their securities should not be considered substantially identical in that too many contingencies exist, or may arise, which might prevent the merger. Even after approval by the stockholders, other contingencies, such as intervention by the federal government, may prevent the merger. However, if the market prices of the stocks are fluctuating proportionately to each other and stockholders' approval of the merger has been obtained, the Treasury might maintain that the stocks of the two corporations are substantially identical to each other.

"When issued" securities of a successor corporation may be substantially identical to the securities to be exchanged for them in a reorganization.[183] However, the Treasury has ruled that where a taxpayer has made a short sale of the "when issued" common stock of a corporation and at the time of the sale holds convertible preferred stock which is not substantially identical to the common, the conversion of the preferred into the common prior to the closing of the short sale does not constitute the acquisition of substantially identical stock.[184] (See page 104 for further discussion of the short sale rules as applicable to "when issued" transactions.)

Common stock is not considered identical to other classes of non-convertible stock or bonds in the same corporation unless there are only minor differences between them. Convertible preferred stock, convertible bonds or warrants are treated as substantially identical to the securities into which they are convertible only when their relative values and price changes have been generally similar to the underlying security.[185] Thus, for example, where the conversion price for the bond is greater than the market price of the underlying security, the price of the bond will be more dependent upon its yield and security than upon the value of its conversion feature. Note, however, should the value of the underlying stock rise above the conversion price, the value of the bond would more

---

182 Reg. 1.1233-1(d)(1)
183 Reg. 1.1233-1(c)(6), example (6)
184 Rev. Rul. 62-153, C.B. 1962-2,186

185 Reg. 1.1233-1(d)(1); Rev. Rul. 77-201, I.R.B. 1977-23, 16

closely reflect its conversion right and its price would fluctuate more uniformly with the underlying security. If the fluctuations in the price of the convertible bond and its underlying security are not uniform, it is questionable whether the securities would be considered as substantially identical.

Bonds issued by the same governmental agency may not be substantially identical if there are different dates of issue, dates of interest payments, maturity dates, callable features or interest rates.[186] In ruling that U.S. Treasury bonds were not substantially identical for wash sale purposes because of different annual interest rates, maturity dates and their use in payment of Federal estate taxes, the Treasury indicated that it may be sufficient if they are substantially different in any material feature.[187]

A Call is not substantially identical to the underlying security for purposes of the short sale rules.[188] Thus, the buying or writing of a Listed Call option would not come within the short sale provisions. This should be true even if the Listed Call, that was written, is deep "in the money" and is, from a practical viewpoint, assured of exercise near the end of the option term. Thus, the taxpayer is extending his holding period on the stock position to obtain long-term capital gain treatment (see page 17).

See page 109 for a discussion of when commodity futures are considered to be "substantially identical."

Short Sale Covered After Death

An unrealized gain or loss on a short sale that remains open at the date of the investor's death is not treated as income in respect of a decedent (Section 691 income).[189] The unrealized amount is not reportable until the short sale has been fully consummated by delivery of the underlying stock by the estate or beneficiary to close the transaction. Prior to enactment of the basis carryover at death provision (see page 65), an investor could escape gain on appreciated securities by not closing a short sale during his lifetime. Since under the former rules the securities received a new tax

---

[186] Rev. Rul. 58-210, C.B. 1958-1, 523; [187] Rev. Rul. 76-346, I.R.B. 1976-37, 9
Rev. Rul. 58-211, C.B. 1958-1, 529; [188] Rev. Rul. 58-384, C.B. 1958-2, 410
Rev. Rul. 59-44, C.B. 1959-1, 205 [189] Rev. Rul. 73-524, C.B. 1973-2, 307

basis, which generally was the amount reported on the decedent's estate tax return, a potential gain could be converted into a loss by closing the short sale after death. For example, assume an investor acquired stock at $50, sold it short at a price of $100, and the value of the stock was $120 at time of death. Closing the short sale after death resulted in a loss of $20 (new tax basis of $120 less sales price of $100), whereas a $50 gain would be included in income if the short sale were closed before death. Note for Federal estate tax purposes the net asset value would be $100. The stock would be valued at $120 and the short sale contract would be shown as a liability of $120. There would also be a receivable from the broker of $100, representing the amount of the short sale.

Under the basis carryover rules, the decedent's tax basis is retained by his estate or beneficiary with certain adjustments. Thus, in the above example, the estate would realize a $50 gain when it closed the short sale. (For purposes of illustrating the rules, the assumption is that the stock was purchased after December 31, 1976 so as not to bring into consideration the "Fresh Start Rule"—See page 64). The effect of the basis carryover provision is to require the decedent's estate or beneficiary to report the deferred gain on the open short-sale into income as if it were Section 691 income. However, because it is not treated as Section 691 income, the estate or beneficiary does not get an income tax deduction under Section 691(c) for the Federal estate tax attributable to the deferred gain. However, the estate tax attributable to the appreciation would be added to basis in computing the gain, thus effectively resulting in a similar conclusion as Section 691(c), as modified.[190] In addition, the fresh start rules on marketable securities held prior to 1977 would cause the appreciation up to December 31, 1976 to escape tax (see page 64).

The above rationale would also apply to a naked short sale where the investor did not own the underlying security at death. Gain or loss on the closing would depend on the cost of the stock acquired to close the short sale.

---

[190] TRA 1976, Section 2005, Code: 691. Code: 691 was amended in two ways in order to more nearly equate the treatment of 691(a) income to carryover basis property. First, the deduction for taxes includes all Federal and State Estate Taxes as defined in Section 1023(f)(3). Second, the average estate tax burden, rather than as in the old law, the incremental top tax burden, is the deduction allowed. This is also similar to the treatment under Section 1023.

For a discussion of the deductibility of dividends and interest paid on a short sale, see page 129. *Dividends and Interest Paid on Short Sales*

The short sale transaction lends itself to use in many situations where planned tax savings can be achieved. See pages 1, 19, 22, 23, 32, 38, 41, and 43. *Tax Savings Opportunities*

PUTS AND CALLS—OPTIONS TO BUY AND SELL SECURITIES

In 1973 Call options started trading on the Chicago Board of Exchange (CBOE). Subsequently, trading of Calls commenced on the American, Philadelphia, Pacific and Midwest Stock Exchanges, with the New York Stock Exchange considering the introduction of option trading. Trading in Puts on a pilot basis was introduced in June 1977. *Introduction*

The discussion that follows will concern itself primarily with the tax implications with respect to transactions in Listed options. However, in most cases the same rules will be applicable to Unlisted options, i.e., those options which are not traded on the various exchanges mentioned above. The existence of different tax rules with respect to Unlisted options will be indicated where appropriate.

Call: A Listed Call is an option to buy 100 shares of a particular stock at a fixed price ("striking price") within a stated period of time, i.e., prior to expiration date. The terms of the Call are fixed, with the only variable being the premium to be paid or received. Ordinary dividends will not affect the striking price on the Listed Call. The terms of an Unlisted Call are not fixed and are determined by negotiation between the buyer and seller. In addition, the rights and obligations are between the buyer and seller and not between a party and the Options Clearing Corp. as with Listed Calls. Furthermore, ordinary dividends will affect the striking price of the Unlisted Call. *Definitions*

Put: A Listed Put is an option to sell 100 shares of a particular stock at a fixed price within a stated period of time. All other aspects discussed above with respect to a Call are applicable to Listed and/or Unlisted Puts.

Straddle: A Straddle is a combination of a Put and Call, both exercisable at the same market price and for the same period.

Combination: A Combination, as the term is used in connection with Listed options, is similar to a Straddle except that the striking price of the Put and Call elements are not the same. (The term "Spread" was previously used for Unlisted options, but such term is now used to describe two or more different Listed Calls with different striking prices and/or maturity dates (see below)).

Strip/Strap: A Strip is a term used to describe a Straddle with a second Put component, whereas a Strap represents a Call plus a Straddle. Both were used prior to the introduction of Listed options.[191]

Time Spread/Calendar Spread/Horizontal Spread: These terms are used for positions in options with different expiration dates and usually the same striking price (e.g., T buys one Call ABC Apr. 40 at $5\frac{1}{2}$ and writes (sells) one Call ABC Jan. 40 at 4, or vice versa). The relationship of the market value of ABC stock to the striking price of the Calls will determine whether the Spread is a Bullish or Bearish Spread.

Vertical Spread/Price Spread/Strike Spread: These terms are used for positions in options with the same expiration date but different striking price (e.g., T buys one Call ABC Jan. 40 at 4 and sells one Call ABC Jan. 45 at 1—Bullish Vertical Spread; or T buys one Call ABC Jan. 45 at 1 and sells one Call ABC Jan. 40 at 4—Bearish Vertical Spread).

Butterfly Spread/Sandwich Spread: These terms are given to positions which combine the Bullish and Bearish Vertical Spreads (e.g., T buys one Call ABC Jan. 40, sells two Calls ABC Jan. 45's, and buys one Call ABC Jan. 50—1:2:1—same maturity).

---

[191] These combinations are referred to as "multiple options" in Reg. 1.1234-2 (b) (4). A grantor is permitted to identify which two of the options constitute a straddle. Reg. 1.1234-2(c)

Domino Spread: This term is given to positions which are similar to the Butterfly Spread, but have different maturity dates.

Intrinsic Value: This term is used to describe the true economic value of the option on the assumption that the option is exercised immediately (e.g., a Call ABC Jan. 25 is selling for a premium of $650, and ABC is selling at $28½ per share. The intrinsic value of the option is $350 or $3½ per share).

Time Value: This term is used to describe the portion of an option's price, above its Intrinsic Value, which represents the value of the time left before it expires (e.g., in the example immediately above, the time value is $3 per share).

Negative Parity: This term is used to describe the occasions where the Intrinsic Value is greater than the total premium which could cause an unwelcome exercise of the option (e.g., On October 1, ABC stock is selling at $45 per share and the premium on an ABC Call—Oct. 35 is $975—$9¾ per share. Professional arbitrageurs might take advantage of the ¼ point spread).

Covered Writing/One-for-One Writing: This terminology is given to a strategy of writing one Call for each 100 shares of stock owned, or in the alternative, writing one Put for each 100 shares of stock sold short.

Uncovered Writing/Naked Options/Short Options: This terminology is given to a strategy of writing Calls without owning the underlying stock, or in the alternative, writing Puts without selling the stock short.

Ratio Writing: This terminology is given to the strategy of writing more than one Call for each 100 shares of stock owned, or in the alternative, writing more than one Put for each 100 shares of stock sold short. In effect, the writer is naked or uncovered as to the number of options in excess of his long position or short position, respectively.

Warrants and purchased stock rights are generally subject to the same tax rules as Calls. For treatment of stock rights received by a shareholder as a distribution, see page 138.

Functions of Options

The most important economic functions of Puts, Calls, etc., are either:

- to provide a means of reducing the risk of loss where an investment or speculation in stock is concerned, or

- to increase the leverage that can be employed.

They may be used as a vehicle for trading the underlying stock against the option or to protect a profit in a position. Certain tax considerations may favor the purchase and/or sale of each option (see pages 5, 17, 19, and 35 through 41). It is important that the cost of the option, all brokerage commissions and transfer taxes (in the purchase of a Call, not applicable to a Put) be considered in any economic or tax planning.

Tax Effect on the Investor Who Purchases an Option

Capital Asset: These options are considered to be capital assets in the hands of the investor [192] and tax treatment depends upon their disposition. The Tax Reform Act of 1976 did not affect the tax treatment to purchasers of options, but only to writers of options (discussed below). The premium paid to acquire an option is carried as a capitalized expenditure made in an incomplete transaction.[193] The ultimate tax treatment will depend upon whether the option is sold, allowed to lapse or exercised.

Sale of Option: If the option is sold, the difference between the cost of the option and the proceeds from the sale is treated as a capital gain or loss. The period for which the investor has held the option determines whether the capital gain or loss is short-term or long-term.[194] Inasmuch as Listed options apparently will not have expiration dates beyond one year, it will be virtually impossible to obtain long-term capital gain or loss treatment on the sale of such options. However, Unlisted options may exist for periods of more than one year and accordingly, long-term treatment may be available.

Failure to Exercise Option: If an option is not exercised, it is treated as having been sold on the expiration date.[195] Therefore, a

---

[192] Code: 1234(a)
[193] Rev. Rul. 71-521, C.B. 1971-2, 313
[194] Reg. 1.1234-1(a)
[195] Code: 1234(a)(2)

Listed option which, as indicated above, will apparently have an expiration date of less than one year, will produce a short-term capital loss. An Unlisted option with an expiration date of more than one year would produce a long-term capital loss. Consideration should be given to the sale of the more than one year Unlisted option before the expiration of the one year holding period if it is expected that the option will not be exercised. This should create a short-term (rather than a long-term) capital loss. Where a Put has been acquired on the same date as the stock which is identified to be used if the Put is exercised so as to come within the exception to the short sale rules ("marriage" of the Put to the stock), then upon expiration of the Put, the cost thereof is not treated as a capital loss, but must be added to the basis of the stock with which it has been identified.[196] (See page 87, and page 94—short sales paragraph under this chapter.)

Exercise of Option: If a Put or Call is exercised, the investor will treat the cost thereof as follows: the amount paid for the Call will increase the cost of the stock acquired, while the amount paid for the Put will decrease the proceeds of sale of the stock sold.[197] Upon the exercise of a Call, the holding period of the stock so acquired does not include the holding period of the Call, but starts the day after the Call is exercised.

Short Sale Rules: The acquisition of a Put is treated as a short sale for purposes of the short sale rules so as to affect the holding period of stock held for less than one year, and the exercise or failure to exercise such Put is considered as a closing of the short sale.[198] (See page 86) Note, the holding period is lost and will not start over again until the Put is disposed of. This is true even though the stock is sold later at a loss. However, if a Put and the stock intended to be used in exercising the Put are acquired on the same day, the short sale rules mentioned above are not applicable, provided the stock is actually so used if the Put is exercised

---

[196] Code: 1233(c)
[197] Rev. Rul. 58-234, C.B. 1958-1, 279
[198] Code: 1233(b); Reg. 1.1233-1(c) (3); Special ruling September 7, 1973, 74-9 CCH ¶6596. This private ruling originally indicated that the sale of the previously purchased Put, would retroactively reinstate the original holding period of the long posi-

tion. A subsequent private ruling dated April 30, 1976 retracted the IRS's original erroneous interpretation of the short sale rules. Thus, the subsequent disposition of an acquired Put will merely start the commencement of the new holding period of the stock.

("marriage" of the Put to the stock) (see page 87). Where an Unlisted Put which has been held for more than one year has increased in value because the market value of the stock has fallen, a sale of the Put would produce long-term capital gain (see example on page 39). However, a question has been raised as to the tax consequences of a sale of the identified or married Put (e.g., at a gain or even to recoup a portion of the investment in the Put). Does such a disposition dissolve the identification or marriage such that the Put, from the beginning, would be treated as a short sale causing the holding period of the stock held less than one year to be lost? The stronger position appears to be that the short sale rules are not activated. Certainly, if the Put is not exercised because the stock has increased in value, the holding period of the "married" stock is not tainted retroactively and such holding period would continue. A sale of the Put has the same effect as the failure to exercise the Put [199] and accordingly, the "married" stock should not be tainted retroactively. Only if the Put is exercised does the identified or married stock have to be delivered. If other stock is delivered, then the short sale rules would activate from the beginning and, if applicable, the holding period of the original identified stock would be lost.

As indicated on page 83, statutory rules have been established with respect to "substantially identical property" in order to prevent the use of short sales to convert short-term gains into long-term gains or to create artificial long-term gains and short-term losses. Property for this purpose includes only stock and securities. A question has been raised as to whether or not options are securities for purposes of the short sale rules. (A similar question exists for purposes of the wash sales rules and for dealers in securities.) If an option is not a security under the short sale rules, it might be possible to effect a short-against-the-box position similar to stock positions (see page 2). Thus, for example, if T purchased on October 15, 1977 an Unlisted one year ten day Call on ABC for $700 and two months later the value of the Call is $2000, T could write an Unlisted Call to expire on the same date as the Call he purchased for $700. He thus would create a short-

---

[199] In interpreting Code: 1233(b), the April 30, 1976 private ruling, referred to in the above footnote 198, stated "For purposes of Section 1233(b), the failure to exercise a Put includes, for example, the lapse of the Put or the sale of the Put." The same conclusion should be reached with respect to the "marriage" provisions of Code: 1233(c)

against-the-box position and by keeping the position open for more than one year, mature the $1,300 locked-in gain into long-term capital gain. If an option is a security, then this conversion cannot occur.

In general: Income is not recognized on the receipt of the premium for writing an option, nor will any gain or loss be recognized until the option is exercised, expires or is terminated by the grantor.

Non-Exercise of Option: Expiration of options issued on or after September 2, 1976 will result in short-term capital gain.[200] The premium received for options granted prior to September 2, 1976 will be treated as ordinary income at the time the option expires unexercised.[201] Recognition of short-term gain under the new rules will enable the writer of the option to offset the gain by capital losses realized in the same taxable year or carried over from prior years. This was not possible under the prior provisions.

Exercise of Option: The stock purchased by the investor upon the exercise of a Put he granted will acquire as a basis the option price paid by him, less the premium received on the writing of the Put.[202] The holding period of such acquired stock begins on the day after the date of the exercise of the option.[203]

For purposes of determining gain or loss, the proceeds from the sale of stock pursuant to the exercise of a Call granted by the investor will be increased by the amount of premium received upon the granting of the Call. If the stock was held by the investor for more than one year, any gain or loss, after including the premium on the granting of the option as part of the proceeds of sale, will be long-term.[204]

Options Repurchased: With the advent of Listed options, it became common practice for owners of stock to write Listed Call options on such stock. If the price of the stock rose, he could terminate the

---

[200] Code: 1234(b)(1), as amended by 1976 TRA: 2136
[201] Rev. Rul. 58-234 C.B. 1958-1, 279
[202] Ibid
[203] Cf. *Weir*, 10 TC 996 (1948)
[204] Rev. Rul. 58-234, C.B. 1958-1, 279

outstanding Call by repurchasing in the open market the identical Call option in a closing transaction. Any gain or loss realized on a closing transaction with respect to options written on or after September 2, 1976 will be treated as short-term capital gain or loss.[205] Gains and losses realized on terminations of options granted prior to September 1, 1976 were accorded ordinary gain or loss treatment.[206]

The potential tax advantage of option writing (long-term capital gain and ordinary loss), that was closed by the Tax Reform Act of 1976, was available primarily when stock prices rose. Many times it resulted in a tax disadvantage in declining markets (i.e., long or short-term capital loss and ordinary income). Thus, many writers of options on a "one-to-one basis" realized a pre-tax reasonable rate of return on invested dollars and mitigated their loss in declining markets, but suffered adverse tax consequences in such declining markets. The new rules eliminate the adverse tax consequences in declining markets and allow a portion of the advantages in rising markets. It is still possible to create long-term capital gain on the stock purchased and short-term capital loss on the option written. To the extent the capital losses are offset against short-term capital gains or ordinary income, a writer of options can obtain the same tax benefit that was previously available before the 1976 TRA. (See page 62.)

The Treasury had previously ruled that a loss incurred on the reacquisition of a Call had to be added to the basis of the underlying stock under certain circumstances.[207] The ruling appears to be contrary in principle with the private ruling which allowed an ordinary deduction under the prior law on the closing of a covered Listed Call transaction. It would also appear that the ruling is contrary to Code Sec. 1234(b) as amended by the Tax Reform Act of 1976. The Treasury has recently revoked the ruling.

Where the premium attributable to the time value of a short Call is very low or where negative parity exists, there might be an un-

---

[205] Code: 1234(b)(1) as amended by 1976 TRA: 2136

[206] Special Ruling, April 8, 1974, 74-9 CCH §6597.

[207] Rev. Rul. 70-205, C.B. 1970-1, 174

welcome exercise of the Call. The writer of the Call should take care to repurchase, in a closing transaction, such short Call with the possible view of rewriting another Call option with a higher striking price and further maturity date. Unwelcome exercises of Calls can occur substantially prior to maturity date, such as when the underlying stock is about to go ex-dividend a significant amount or buyers of the underlying stock are interested in large acquisitions without significantly affecting the price, or for other reasons. The investor may not have owned the underlying stock for more than one year and unwelcome exercise and delivery of the underlying stock would cause any gain to be short-term capital gain. If newly purchased stock is used to satisfy the exercised Call, it could be argued that stock is borrowed temporarily by the broker on behalf of the investor for delivery in satisfaction of the exercised Call and that, in effect, the equivalent of a short sale for tax purposes has occurred, with the resulting loss of holding period on the long position that was held for less than one year. Such an argument appears to be far-fetched inasmuch as a conscious short sale should be required in order to activate the short sale rules and not merely a temporary borrowing in the satisfaction of an exercised Call until the newly purchased stock can be used to satisfy the exercised Call.

Wash Sales

Where an investor sells stock or securities at a loss and within a thirty day period before or after such sale, acquires (or enters into an option to acquire) substantially identical securities, the loss will be disallowed as a wash sale.[208] Thus, the acquisition of a Call within thirty days before or after the sale of stock or securities at a loss will cause the loss to be disallowed. The authors believe that the loss and the holding period of the stock sold should be added to the basis and holding period of the option acquired (see page 77).[209] If the Call is subsequently exercised, the basis of the new stock would effectively include the total basis of the Call, i.e., the cost of the Call plus the disallowed loss on the original stock position. The holding period of the new stock should not include the holding period of the option nor the holding period of the original stock position because of the general rule that the total holding period of the option upon exercise is lost.[210]

---

[208] Code: 1091(a)
[209] Reg. 1.1091-1(a)

[210] Code: 1223(4). A literal reading of

If the Call expires unexercised, the loss should be equal to the tax basis of the Call, i.e., the cost of the Call plus the disallowed loss attributable to the original stock and the nature of the gain should depend upon the total holding period of the Call.

As indicated previously, it is not clear whether an option is deemed to be a security for purposes of the wash sale rules. Thus, the sale of a Listed option at a loss with a subsequent repurchase within thirty days of the identical Listed option will cause the wash sale rules to apply only if such option is deemed to be a "security" within Section 1091. Options with different maturity dates and/or different striking prices should not be substantially identical to each other so as to come within the wash sale rules.

The purchase of a Listed option "to close" at a loss with a subsequent resale within thirty days of the identical Listed option is not a wash sale, because you generally need two purchases and one sale to come within Section 1091, and under these circumstances, there are two sales and only one purchase.

If the individual investor's activities are sufficient enough such that he is considered to be a trader, he would be exempt from the wash sale provisions.[211]

A sale of a Call at a loss with a purchase of the stock within the thirty day period is not a wash sale (see page 78).

Dividends and Other Rights Paid during Period of Unlisted Options Both Unlisted Calls and Puts usually provide that the option price will be reduced by the value of any distributions (cash dividends, stock dividends, warrants, etc.) received on the stock during the life of the option. In such cases, all dividends, to the extent taxable, are includible in the gross income of the owner of the stock when its holder receives the dividend.[212] The adjustment to the

---

Section 1091(d) (basis provision) and Section 1223(4) (holding period provision) could lead to the conclusion that the disallowed loss and the holding period of the stock sold are not added to the basis and holding period of the option. In addition, if the option is exercised, the disallowed loss is then effectively added to the basis of the new stock, and the holding period of the old stock, but not the holding period of the option, is tacked onto the holding period of the new stock. These literal interpretations appear to be strained and contrary to legislative intent, espeically where the options are not exercised.

[211] Reg. 1.1091-1(a)

[212] Ibid.; see generally I.T. 4007, C.B. 1950-1, 11 (superseded by Rev. Rul. 74-562, C.B. 1974-2, 28); Rev. Rul. 56-153, CB 1956-1, 166; and Rev. Rul. 56-211, C.B. 1956-1, 155

sales price affects only the tax basis of the stock acquired on the exercise of the option and has no other tax effect.[213] The option price of Listed Puts and Calls is not affected by ordinary dividends.

Listed Straddles: Transactions on Listed Puts and Calls with the same striking price and expiration date may be considered as a transaction in Straddles. The writing of such Listed options does not create an allocation problem that existed and probably still exists with respect to Unlisted Straddles inasmuch as the separate components of the "Listed Straddles" will be known, i.e., the Listed Call and Listed Put are traded separately on the exchange. **Straddles**

Unlisted Straddles: Prior rulings and cases will be relevant with respect to Unlisted Straddles and Spreads. The premium received by an investor for writing a Straddle must be allocated based upon the market values (at the time the Straddle was written) of the Unlisted Put and Unlisted Call options contained therein.[214] In lieu of determining the market values of the two options, the taxpayer may elect by a statement attached to his income tax return to allocate 55 percent of the premium to the Call option and 45 percent to the Put option, provided that these ratios (or subsequently announced ratios) are used in allocating all future premiums received in writing Straddles.[215] The premium applicable to the unexpired option will be treated as short-term capital gain upon its expiration.[216] The premium allocated to the exercised portion of the Straddle will reduce the cost of stock acquired or increase the proceeds of sale of the stock sold, depending upon

---

[213] Rev. Rul. 58-234, C.B. 1958-1, 279

[214] Rev. Rul. 65-31, C.B. 1965-1, 365. It had been the practice of most taxpayers who wrote Straddles to allocate the entire premium received to the side of the option exercised. In recognition of that prevailing practice, the ruling applies only to straddles written after January 25, 1965. Similar rules are contained in Reg. 1.1234-2(d). Despite the deletion of Section 1234(c) by the 1976 TRA, it is expected that the Treasury will require the same method of allocating premiums on straddles written after September 1, 1976.

[215] Rev. Proc. 65-29, C.B. 1965-2, 1023

[216] Code: 1234(c) (applicable to Straddles written after January 25, 1965 and before September 2, 1976). Section 1234(c) was deleted from the Code by the 1976 TRA because grantors of options now realize short-term capital gain on lapse of options and therefore it is no longer necessary to have a special short-term capital gain provision for writers of Straddles. Under the pre-1976 TRA rules the premium applicable to the unexercised portion of a Spread written before September 2, 1976, or to any unexercised part of a Strip or Strap not identified as part of a Straddle, will be treated as ordinary income to the writer when the option expires. Reg. 1.1234-2(f), Example (7). Again, these gains will be short-term for multiple options written on or after September 1, 1976.

whether the Call or the Put option was exercised. If both options lapse, the premiums would be taxed as short-term gain.[217]

With respect to Straddles or other combinations of Unlisted Puts and Calls acquired by the investor, theoretically the exercise of one side of the contract should not affect the status of the unexercised portion. The part of the cost of the Straddle applicable to the unexercised option should be treated as a sale of that option on the expiration date. Thus, if the Call is exercised, the cost of the Straddle applicable to such buy option would be added to the basis of the stock acquired, while the cost attributable to the Put would result in a capital loss upon its expiration. Many investors have in the past taken the position that the entire cost of the Straddle should be allocated to the portion exercised. However, in light of the Treasury's position with respect to the writing of a Straddle, a separate allocation will be required.[218]

If the Unlisted Call portion of an Unlisted Straddle is exercised, the stock so acquired will not receive a holding period until the Unlisted Put portion either is sold or expires, since the Put will be considered an open short sale and thus taint the holding period of the newly acquired long position. The holding period thus commences when the short sale is considered covered. It is therefore recommended that if the Put portion of a Straddle has any time remaining before its expiration date and is of no immediate value to the investor, the Put should be disposed of in order to allow the holding period of the newly acquired stock to commence.

Options on Commodity Futures (Double Options) Trading in options on commodity futures has been prevalent in Europe for many years and has been available in the United States in a small way. It is expected, in the near future, that such option trading will be permitted in the United States under stringent regulatory control and will become as important to commodity future trading as Listed options is to stock trading today.

---

[217] Reg. 1.1234-2(f), Example (3). The Treasury reversed its prior position in Prop. Reg. 1.1234-2(a) that the lapse would be taxed as ordinary income. The final regulations corresponds more closely with the literal language of old Section 1234(c) and is the same treatment accorded under the 1976 TRA.

[218] Reg. 1.1234-2(f), Example 1

The purchases and sales of Puts and Calls (i.e., long a Put, long a Call, short a Put and short a Call) prior to September 2, 1976 could have resulted in net ordinary loss (in closing transactions in both the short Put and short Call) and net capital gain (on the sales of both the long Put and the long Call) provided there was sufficient movement in the underlying commodity future. The pretax economics of the several transactions and strategy depended upon the magnitude in price movement of the underlying commodity future, the amount paid for the purchased options compared to the premiums received for the sold options and the timing relevant to disposition of the various segments of the transactions. Similar options written after September 1, 1976 will result in short-term capital gain or loss upon the closing transactions. The one-year holding requirement will be applicable to commodity futures options purchases and not the six month period applicable to commodity futures transactions.

"WHEN ISSUED" TRANSACTIONS

Nature of Trans-actions

When an investor buys or sells securities "when issued," he actually contracts to purchase or sell the securities "when, as and if issued," and for tax purposes there is no purchase or sale until the securities are issued.[219] An investor who buys and subsequently sells securities on a "when issued" basis is technically acquiring two contracts. When these contracts are cleared on the settlement date, the sale and exchange of the securities is deemed to take place on such date. Thus all gains or losses realized in such matching transactions are short-term.[220] When the investor holds several blocks of "old" securities, has sold at various times the "new" securities on a "when issued" basis and cannot identify sales with specific acquisitions (see page 75), the gains or losses on the transactions are measured by matching the earliest "when issued" sales with the securities sold in order of their dates of acquisition.[221] Options written on "when issued" securities are treated the same as options written on issued securities. See page 94 through page 100 for tax treatment of purchasers and writers of options.[222]

[219] *Walker,* 35 BTA 640 (1937) (A)

[220] *Shanis,* 19 T.C. 641 (1953), aff'd per curiam 213 F. 2d 151 (CA-3, 1954) : IT 3721, C.B. 1945, 164

[221] *Haynes,* 17 T.C. 772 (1952) (A)

[222] Code: 1234(b) (2) (B) as amended by 1976 TRA: 2136.

Wash Sale Rules A loss sustained as of the settlement date of the "when issued" contracts will be disallowed if substantially identical securities are acquired within 30 days of that settlement date.[223] For this purpose, securities acquired under "when issued" contracts are deemed to be acquired on the settlement date. (See page 81 for further discussion of the wash sale rules and their inapplicability where sales are made in a bona fide reduction of holdings acquired within 30 days.)

Short Sales A "when issued" security is considered property for purposes of the short sale rules.[224] Therefore the acquisition of a "when issued" security and the short sale of the "old" security or vice versa, where both are substantially identical, will cause the short sale rules to apply. (See page 83 for further discussion of the short sale rules.)

Holding Period of Securities Originally Purchased "When Issued" If the actual securities are received pursuant to the "when issued" contract, the investor's holding period for the "new" securities will start from the settlement date and not when the "when issued" contract was acquired.[225] Thus, a sale of the "new" securities at a gain immediately after the receipt thereof would result in short-term gain even if the "when issued" contract had been held for more than one year.

Sale of Contract The Treasury has ruled that a sale or exchange of a "when issued" contract itself is the sale or exchange of a capital asset resulting in gain or loss.[226] Thus, it is theoretically possible to sell a contract to buy "when issued" stock which has been held for more than one year and have the gain treated as long-term.[227] According to the same ruling, an identical result could be achieved by selling a contract to sell securities "when issued." [228] Although the Treasury ruling apparently remains in effect, there is a possibility that the Treasury would contend that the subsequently enacted short sales rules (see page 83) prevent the long-term capital gain treatment.[229]

---

[223] IT 3858, C.B. 1947-2, 71; however, cf. Rev. Rul. 56-602, C.B. 1956-2, 527

[224] Reg. 1.1233-1(c)(1)

[225] IT 3721, C.B. 1945, 164; question (e) at page 173

[226] IT 3721, C.B. 1945, 164; Rev. Rul. 57-29, C.B. 1957-1, 519

[227] Ibid

[228] Ibid; see also *Stavisky*, 34 T.C. 140

(1960), aff'd 291 F.2d 48 (CA-2, 1961)

[229] See Sen. Rep. No. 2375, 81st Con., 2nd Sess. p. 87, C.B. 1950-2, 483, 545. The Treasury's failure to reflect in the regulations this committee report indicating that the assignment of a "when issued" contract is equivalent to the closing of a short sale, together with

Practical Limitations: An attempt to sell a contract to buy or a contract to sell securities "when issued" through a stockbroker may be frustrated in that the stockbroker, applying the stock exchange rules, will consider the sale of a contract to buy "when issued" as an open sale of the "when issued" securities. Similarly, an attempted sale of the contract to sell securities "when issued" will be considered a purchase of the "when issued" securities. Thus two positions, one long, the other short, will remain open until the settlement date. It is possible that the transaction will never be consummated, thus causing all trades to be cancelled.[230] Perhaps the only solution therefore is a private assignment of the contracts.[231]

In lieu of transferring all the rights under a "when issued" contract, if the investor could obtain a release from and cancellation of the contract itself by a payment to the other party, it may be contended that ordinary loss would result instead of capital loss. However, a payment to a third party to assume a "when issued" contract to sell has been held to result in capital loss.[232]

Payment for Release from "When Issued" Contract

If the transaction contemplated in a "when issued" contract, such as a reorganization, does not take place so that the "when issued" contract becomes worthless, it is believed that the cost of the contract, such as commissions, may be taken as an ordinary deduction.

Worthlessness of "When Issued" Contract

COMMODITY FUTURES

A commodity future is a contract to purchase or sell a fixed amount of a commodity at a future date for a fixed price.[233] The exchange on which the futures are traded specifies certain essential terms of the contract.

Definition

---

its virtual reaffirmation of I.T. 3721, Rev. Rul. 57-29, C.B. 1957-1, 519, would make it very difficult for the Treasury to deny long-term capital gain treatment. In *Stavisky*, 34 T.C. 140, aff'd 291 F. 2d 48, the Tax Court had an opportunity to discuss whether or not the short sale rules apply in this situation, but avoided the issue because the transaction took place prior to the effective date of the short sale rules. Under the facts of the case, the Court ruled a loss on the transfer of a short position in the "when issued" securities to be long-term capital loss.

[230] See *Stavisky*, 291 F. 2d 48 (CA-2, 1961)

[231] Ibid

[232] Ibid

[233] *Corn Products Refining Co.*, 350 U.S. 46 (1955), fn 1.

Transactions in commodity futures generally fall into four classifications:

(1) Hedge transactions used to insure against losses caused by fluctuations in price of a commodity, included in inventory or contracted for future delivery, to be used or sold in the course of business. Such transactions will invariably give rise to ordinary income or loss treatment and therefore are not further considered here.

(2) Nonhedge transactions entered into for speculation or investment purposes with a view towards making a profit. Such transactions will generally generate capital gain or loss.

(3) Straddle transactions, whereby a simultaneous purchase and sale of two commodity futures contracts on the same exchange but requiring delivery in different months, with the expectation of realizing gain through the variation of the prices of the futures contracts as a result of market conditions. Capital gain or loss will generally result from these transactions.

(4) A "cash and carry" transaction, whereby there is a simultaneous purchase of a "spot" commodity contract requiring present delivery of the commodity (or purchase of the nearest month future contract with expectation of taking delivery of the contract) and a sale of a futures contract with the expectation of realizing an overall gain due to a change in interest rates and other economic factors on the subsequent delivery of the commodity upon the closing of the future contract. The expenses incurred while the commodity is stored in a warehouse should be an ordinary deduction and a capital gain will be realized upon the closing of the futures contract.

Tax Consequences

In General: Futures contracts which are not hedges are generally treated as capital assets and gain or loss therefrom will generally be accorded capital gain or loss treatment. In the usual case, a commodity futures contract is held for not more than six months because of market fluctuations and therefore most gains and losses realized by the investor are short-term in nature. However, the sale of a "long" commodity futures contract which is held for more than six months results in long-term capital gain or loss.

The more than six month holding period rule remains in effect for future transactions in any commodity subject to the rules of a board of trade or commodity exchange.[234] However, the longer holding period rules will apply to a sale of a commodity, as distinguished from a commodity futures contract, even if the commodity is used to close the futures transaction. For example, if in July 1977 an investor buys a spot commodity contract, and sells a futures contract which requires delivery after the seventh month, the closing of the futures contract with the spot commodity will be subject to the general rules in effect for 1978. A sale of a Call, Put or other security option will also fall under the general rules even if the option is with respect to a security that is sold over a commodity exchange.

Offsetting trades through the same broker in the same agricultural commodity future (e.g., wheat, eggs, corn, etc.) in the *same market* for the delivery in the *same contract period* are closed as of the moment the offsetting trade is made, pursuant to the rules of the Commodity Exchange Authority[235] and gain or loss is recognized at that time. Where the offsetting trade is made through a different broker, the transaction is not closed. Therefore, "long" and "short" positions are established and gain or loss is recognized only when the positions are covered.[236] Offsetting trades in non-agricultural commodity futures (e.g., copper, zinc, etc.) may not be required to be closed by the exchange on which they are traded. Here also "long" and "short" positions are established and gain or loss is recognized only when the positions are covered.[237]

In determining the holding period of a commodity received in satisfaction of the commodity futures contract, the holding period of the commodity future will be tacked on.[238]

---

[234] Code: 1222. The retention of the more than 6 month holding period with respect to commodity futures was intended to be limited to agricultural commodity futures contracts. Conference Committee Report TRA 1402; Joint Committee explanation, page 508. However, the House language was adopted covering all commodity futures. The IRS announced that all commodity futures are covered by the 6 month rule. News Release IR 1787, (3/30/77.) Proposed prospective legislation would limit the 6 month holding period to agricultural commodity futures contracts.

[235] Commodity Exchange Authority Rules, Section 1.46(a)

[236] Reg. 1.1233-1(d) (2) (iii). The Treasury had ruled, prior to the enactment of the short sale rules (Section 1233), that gain or loss must be recognized at the moment an offsetting trade is made in the same commodity future on the same market for delivery in the same contract period, even if the offsetting trade is made through a different broker. Mim 6243, C.B. 1948-1, 44 (obsolete); Mim 6789, C.B. 1952-1, 38 (obsolete); however cf. *Joseph Maloney*, 25 T.C. 1219 (1956). These rulings apparently have no current effect in light of the applicability of the short sale rules to commodity futures and the example given in Reg. 1.1233-1(d) (2) (iii).

[237] Ibid

[238] Code: 1223(8)

Straddles: As indicated below, a purchase of a commodity future requiring delivery in one calendar month and a simultaneous sale of a commodity future requiring delivery in another calendar month do not fall within the short sale rules. Therefore, an investor may avail himself of this statutory exception when entering into this transaction for profit, to realize a short-term capital loss in the current taxable year and possible long-term capital gain in the succeeding year. See page 23 for an illustration of the tax savings opportunities available with the utilization of Straddles.

However, the Treasury has ruled that the short-term capital loss generated in a silver Straddle transaction is not an economic loss and is not deductible.[239] The ruling further indicates that the net economic loss, after merging two years' transactions, is not deductible. This revenue ruling has far-reaching effects. The Treasury's utilization of a broad "substance over form" concept and a "lack of real economic loss" concept could cause many transactions, in addition to commodity Straddles, to be challenged. There is no effective date to this ruling and accordingly, it could be applied to any commodity Straddle or similar transaction as long as the tax year is still open.

It is naturally essential that transactions be entered into with an expectation of realizing a profit, but for the Treasury to present the arguments it made in the ruling and expect that a fair administration of the tax law could be based on such arguments seems unrealistic. The Treasury seems to abandon the distinction between unrealized income and realization and recognition of income, and the concept that each year stands on its own, especially with respect to the proper timing of income for a cash basis taxpayer. The conclusion of the ruling also appears to be erroneous because the Treasury has not fully considered the economics and profit potential of commodity Straddle transactions. An investor, for example, in a silver Straddle, who is long the near month future and short the far month future will realize a significant pre-tax profit if interest rates drop, causing the spread between the contracts to narrow. An inversion (i.e., the further out silver future falling in price below the nearer term silver future) will result in a substantial pre-tax profit in relationship to the amount of invested capital.

---

[239] Rev. Rul. 77-185, I.R.B. 1977-21, 7

Prior to the 1976 TRA an investor could realize an ordinary loss on commodity transactions by buying and selling a Call and a Put in a commodity. An ordinary loss was allowed when he closed his option he had written at a loss similar to the Listed options rule. (See page 97.) However, a similar transaction would now result in a short term loss.[240] An ordinary loss can still be realized in a commodity contract by means of a "cash and carry" transaction discussed below.

Cash and Carry: A "cash and carry" transaction is similar to a commodity Straddle except that the investor purchases a "spot" commodity contract in lieu of a future contract and takes delivery of the commodity, ordinarily through a warehouse receipt. (The investor could also purchase the nearest month future contract and take delivery of the commodity.) He simultaneously sells a commodity future requiring delivery, preferably more than one year out. The investor hopes to make money in this transaction due to expectations of changes in interest rates and other costs of carrying the spot commodity, when compared to the "locked in" spread between the cost of the spot and the selling amount of the futures contract. Silver, gold and other metals lend themselves to the cash and carry transactions. However, care must be taken to be sure that the proper spread exists and other economic conditions are favorable before entering into the transaction. The expenses for storage, insurance and interest on borrowed funds to purchase the commodity should be deductible against ordinary income.[241] The closing of the short position with the commodity held in storage is not a short sale,[242] and, therefore, would result in long term capital gain if held for more than one year (the six month holding period rule applies only to commodity futures.[243]) Short term gain would result from the closing of the "short" position by buying a "long" position with the same delivery date.

Short Sales: Under the short sale rules (see page 83) a commodity future requiring delivery in one calendar month is not substantially

---

[240] Code: 1234(b) as amended by 1976 TRA; 2136

[241] C. A. Higgins, 75 Fed. Supp. 252 (Ct. Cls. 1948), *Heaven Hill Distilleries, Inc.,* 476 F. 2d 1327 (Ct. Cls. 1973); not followed where storage improved whiskey, *George L. Schultz,*

50 T.C. 688 (1968), aff'd. per curiam 420 F. 2d 490 (CA-3, 1970); Rev. Rul. 70-356, C.B. 1970-2, 68

[242] Code: 1233(e)

[243] Code: 1222 as amended by 1976 TRA: 1402(d)

identical to another future in the same commodity requiring delivery in a different calendar month.[244] Thus, the regulations indicate that commodity futures in May and July wheat are not substantially identical and, therfore, the short sale rules are not applicable.[245] The short sale rules also do not apply to futures which trade in different markets even though they are substantially identical if offsetting transactions are entered into on the same day and both are closed on the same day.[246] Whether futures in the same commodity traded in different markets are substantially identical will depend upon the facts and circumstances. According to the regulations, historical similarity in price movements in the two markets is the primary factor to be considered.[247] An investor who has sold a commodity future short is precluded from enjoying any long-term capital gain upon closing the short sale by buying in the commodity future because of the short sale rules.[248] Note that for purposes of the short sale rule, property includes only commodity futures, and therefore the use of a commodity to close the commodity future would not fall within the provinces of the short sale provisions.[249]

Wash Sale Rules: The courts are in conflict both as to whether the wash sale provisions apply to commodity futures transactions and, if so, whether futures contracts with different delivery dates are "substantially identical" for purposes of the wash sale rules.[250] However, the Treasury has ruled that the wash sale rules do not apply to commodity futures.[251] As mentioned previously, for purposes of the short sale rules the latter type of contracts are not "substantially identical." [252] (See page 77 for discussion of wash sale rules.)

TREASURY BILL FUTURES

Description: In 1976 the Chicago Board of Trade began trading futures contracts on Treasury bills in a manner similar to commodity futures. The futures market is intended to provide a hedge against the volatility in interest rates for owners of substantial

---

[244] Code: 1233(e)(2)(B)
[245] Reg. 1.1233-1(d)(2)(i)
[246] Code: 1233(e)(3)
[247] Reg. 1.1233-1(d)(2)(i)
[248] Code: 1233(a); Sen. Rep. No. 2375, 81st Cong. 2nd Sess. p. 87 C.B. 1950-2, 483, p. 545; cf. *Joseph Maloney*, 25 T.C. 1219 (1956)
[249] Code: 1233(e)(2)(A)
[250] *Trenton Cotton Oil Co.*, 147 F. 2d 33

(CA-6, 1945); *Corn Products Refining Co.*, 16 T.C. 395, aff'd on other issues 350 U.S. 46; *Sicanoff Vegetable Oil Corp.*, 27 T.C. 1056 (1957) rev'd on other issues 251 F. 2d 764 (CA-7, 1958)
[251] Rev. Rul. 71-568, C.B. 1971-2, C.B. 312
[252] Code: 1233(e)(2)(B)

amount of Treasury bills or similar indebtedness. Many investors have taken simultaneous "long" and "short" positions in Treasury bill futures (different months) in the expectation of deriving economic profit from the transaction and, for tax purposes, ordinary losses similar to the treatment of Listed options prior to the 1976 TRA.

Definition: A Treasury bill future, like a commodity future, is a contract to purchase or sell a fixed amount of Treasury bills at a future date for a fixed amount. The basic trading unit is $1 million of face value of Treasury bills maturing in 90 days up to 24 months.

Tax Consequences: Some tax commentators have likened a Treasury bill future to a commodity future and concluded that the termination of a future would result in capital gain or loss (see page 106). However, an important distinction is that, unlike a commodity future, the underlying property is not a capital asset.[253] While a Treasury bill future is technically not excluded from the definition of a capital asset, another analogy would be to compare a Treasury bill future with an option to buy or sell Treasury bills. A sale of an option would result in ordinary income or loss to the purchaser.[254] On the other hand, a purchase by the writer to close the short position would result in short-term gain or loss to the writer.[255] Despite a contrary decision reached by its Manhattan office, the Treasury has recently ruled that a Treasury bill future is a capital asset, resulting in capital gain or loss on its sale.[255a] Under the Treasury's capital gain or loss interpretation, an investor with a short position could obtain an ordinary loss by delivering a Treasury bill in closing the contract. An investor with a long position, who would otherwise realize a capital loss on the sale of the futures contract, could obtain an ordinary loss by taking delivery of the Treasury bill in satisfaction of the futures contract and selling it at a loss. It should also be noted that in the ruling the Treasury bill futures contracts were also treated as commodity futures for purposes of the 6-month holding period for long-term capital gain treatment.

Assuming ordinary gain or loss is recognized on disposition of a Treasury bill future, whether the future is a long or short position,

---

[253] Code: 1221(5)

[254] Code: 1234(a) as amended by the 1976 TRA: 2136

[255] Code: 1234(b) as amended by the 1976 TRA: 2136

[255a] Rev. Rul. 78-414. The principles of Rev. Rul. 77-185 was held to be also applicable to Treasury bill straddles. (See pages 23 and 108.)

an investor could take a Straddle position. Before year-end, the investor would sell the loss position and recognize an ordinary loss. Ordinary income would be realized when its remaining position is closed in the succeeding year (see page 30). (However, the ordinary income treatment is contrary to Rev. Rul. 78-414 and the Straddle transaction may be disallowed under the rationale of Rev. Rul. 77-185.) (See pages 23 and 108.) The use of a Straddle should be limited to special situations. If an investor with a large salary or other personal service income were to enter into a Straddle in order to reduce his personal service income, he would be reducing income subject to a tax of 50 percent and the ordinary income realized in the subsequent year could be subject to tax at rates up to 70 percent.

Note, however, that a Straddle would be more beneficial if it is in the form of options to buy and sell Treasury bills. As discussed above, a purchaser of an option to acquire Treasury bills receives ordinary income or loss treatment on disposition, whereas a writer of the option receives short-term gain or loss treatment on disposition. Accordingly, option spreads might be available with respect to Treasury bills with the possibility of obtaining similar desired results previously available with respect to pre-September 2, 1976 Listed options (i.e., ordinary loss and short-term capital gain—see page 91). The short-term gain element might be converted into long-term by means of investments in commodity Straddles (see page 23).

BONDS

General Rules A bond, like stock, is generally considered to be a capital asset in the hands of an investor. The rules for stock are also applicable to bonds: such as basis, holding period requirements, wash sale rules, etc. Purchase commissions and similar expenses of acquiring bonds are included as part of the cost of acquisition; however, the amount paid on account of accrued interest is not included in the basis of the bond, but must be offset against the first payment of interest income.

Amortization of Bond Premiums *Wholly Tax-Exempt Bonds:* The investor is required to amortize the premium on wholly tax-exempt bonds for the purposes of computing basis,[256] however, no deduction for such amortization is allowable.[257] For state income tax purposes many states do not

---

[256] Reg. 1.1016-5(b)   [257] Code: 171(a)(2)

112

require the bond premium to be amortized if the interest income is subject to state tax. Front load fees charged for the purchase of shares of municipal bond funds or Massachusetts trusts taxed as corporations, should not be amortized since they are incurred in the purchase of a stock interest and not in the purchase of a direct interest in a tax-exempt bond. Therefore, the unamortized amount should be taken into account in reporting gain or loss on a subsequent disposition. A similar treatment may not be applicable to front load fees charged in acquiring municipal bond trust interests. The purchaser is treated for tax purposes as the owner of the property and must report income and deductions as if the grantor owned the property directly. Accordingly, fees incurred in acquiring tax exempts would have to be amortized over the life of the bonds and the amortization would not be deductible since attributable to tax exempt income. Any unamortized fees would be taken into account in determining gain or loss on a premature disposition of the trust interest.

Other Bonds: Investors who elect to amortize bond premiums paid in acquiring fully taxable bonds will be allowed an amortization deduction in computing taxable income (and must make a corresponding negative basis adjustment to the tax basis of the bonds), provided the optional tax tables or the standard deduction are not used in that year.[258] However, an amortization deduction will be deemed to have been taken in the standard deduction year for purposes of computing the adjusted tax basis of the bonds.[259] The binding election applies to all such bonds owned in the year of the election and to such bonds acquired in subsequent years. It is made by claiming the deduction in the return for the taxable year in question.[260] A separate election may be made by the estate, or donee if the investor desires to make a lifetime gift.[261] If the decedent dies before the accrued interest is received, the decedent may still take an amortization deduction on the final tax return although the interest income will be reported by his estate or beneficiaries.[262] An investor who has not received any interest in the taxable year is permitted but not required to deduct the amortization.[263]

The total premium to be amortized with respect to any fully taxable bond acquired after 1957 is the excess of the basis of the bond for

---

[258] Code: 171(a)(1)
[259] Reg. 1.171-1(b)(5)
[260] Reg. 1.171-3

[261] Code: 171(c)
[262] Reg. 1.171-(c)
[263] Reg. 1.171-2(e)

determining loss on a sale or exchange over the amount payable at maturity or any earlier call date, whichever produces the lower tax deduction.[264] See page 64 for determination of basis. Where a premium exists as the result of the addition to the basis of the interest equalization tax paid (see page 139) such premium is amortizable.[265] Special rules apply to premiums on bonds acquired before 1958.[266] The amortizable premium on a bond does not include that part of the premium which is attributable to the conversion features of the bond, determined as of the time of acquisition.[267] The premium attributable to the period prior to the beginning of amortization may not be amortized, but remains part of the basis of the bond to be taken into account in determining gain or loss on disposition. Where the bond is called before maturity and a portion of the premium has not been amortized, the remaining premium may be deducted in the year the bond is called.[268] Note, however, on a sale of the bond, the unamortized premium remains part of the adjusted tax basis in computing gain or loss on the disposition. In the case where the bonds are not called on the call date and the premium has not been fully amortized, the remaining premium is adjusted over the period to the next call date or maturity date.[269]

Amortization of Bond Discount

Investors owning noninterest-bearing obligations issued at a discount and redeemable for fixed amounts increasing at stated intervals, such as Series "E" U.S. savings bonds, may elect to report each year the annual increment in value as income received.[270] Without the election, the investor would report the bunched amount of income when the bond is redeemed. The election is binding as to all such obligations owned or thereafter acquired and for all subsequent years. In the year of election, all increases in redemption value as of the beginning of the year must also be included in income.

---

[264] Code: 171(b)(1)(B)—The premium on callable tax-exempt bonds must be amortized to the "earlier" call date determined under Reg. 1.171-2(b).

[265] See Senate Finance Committee report, P.L. 88-563, section .05(c)(3)

[266] Code: 171(b)(1)(B); Reg. 1.171-2(a)(2)

[267] Code: 171(b(1); Reg. 1.171-2(c)

[268] Reg. 1.171-2(a)(2)(iii)

[269] Reg. 1.171-2(b)(2)

[270] Code: 454(a). This election is not available with respect to savings certificates issued by banks, savings and loans associations and similar organizations. Interest (or "dividends") on such certificates is held to be taxable when there is a right to withdraw it even if the principal must be withdrawn at the same time. (Rev. Rul. 66-44, C.B. 1966-1, 94; Rev. Rul. 66-45, C.B. 1966-1, 95). See also Footnote 271, infra.

In the case of all other types of obligations, other than corporate obligations issued after May 27, 1969, bond discount is not given any tax effect until the obligation is redeemed or otherwise disposed of. For corporate obligations issued after May 27, 1969, the original issue discount must be included in the investor's income on a ratable monthly basis over the life of the obligation.[271] A subsequent holder is required to amortize the remaining discount, less any amount paid for the obligation over the original issue price as increased by prior amortized discount. The basis of the obligation is increased by the bond discount included in income.[272]

Accrued Interest on Purchase or Sale

The amount paid for a bond purchased between interest payment dates will generally include the interest earned to the date of purchase. The investor will reduce his first interest received by this amount.[273] When the bonds are sold, the portion of the proceeds attributable to interest earned to the date of the sale will be reported as interest income.[274] In practice, settlement dates are used in determining the amount of accrued interest.

Interest Income

Interest income may be classified in two types, fully taxable and fully tax-exempt (partially tax-exempt bonds are no longer in existence). Most interest income from corporate bonds and federal bonds falls within the first classification. Interest on obligations of a state or other local authority, the District of Columbia, or a territory or possession of the United States generally is fully exempt from federal tax.[275] Tax-exempt interest may also be received from partnerships or trusts and in taxable years beginning after 1975 from municipal bond funds.[276] Interest on tax-free covenant bonds issued before 1934 by certain corporations is fully taxable, but a credit against tax liability of 2 percent of the interest is allowed to the taxpayer.[277] In determining which type of obligation gives the largest return, the comparison should be based on receipts after taxes.

---

[271] Code: 1232(a)(3). "Other evidence of indebtedness" includes certificates of deposits, time deposits, bonus plans, and other deposit arrangements with banks. Reg. 1.1232-1(d)

[272] Code: 1232(a)(3)(E)

[273] *Thompson Scenic Railway,* 9 BTA 1203 (1928); Sol. Op. 46, 3 C.B. 90 (obsolete)

[274] Reg. 1.61-7(d)

[275] Code: 103. Certain "industrial development" bonds issued after May 1, 1968 and "arbitrage" bonds issued after October 9, 1969 are no longer tax-exempt. Code: 103(c) and (d)

[276] Code: 852(b)(5) as amended by 1976 TRA: 2137(c)

[277] Code: 32(2)

Flat Bonds Many bonds which are in default of interest or principal are traded "flat." The quoted price covers not only the principal, but gives the purchaser the right to unpaid accrued interest without any additional or separate charge. Payments of interest accrued prior to the date of purchase are treated as recovery of cost,[278] while payments attributable to interest earned after such date constitute interest income. If the payment of prepurchase date interest exceeds the basis of the bonds to the investor, the excess is taxed as proceeds of redemption, usually capital gain.[279] Where bonds are sold "flat," the portion of the proceeds attributable to the interest accrued after the date of purchase to the date of sale will be treated as interest income, not as giving rise to capital gain or loss.[280]

Where bonds, which are trading flat, are sold short, a question is raised as to the treatment to the short seller of the payments in lieu of interest that are subsequently made by him. The rule should be similar to payments in lieu of dividends on short sales (see page 129), i.e., deductible as a non-business expense.[281] However, a profit motive must exist in order for the deduction to be sustained.[282] The repurchase of the short position immediately subsequent to the payment of the "flat" interest will result generally in a short-term capital gain equal to the reduction in value of the flat bond.

Retirement Redemption and Disposition of Bonds *General Rule:* The retirement of a bond will be considered as the sale or exchange of that bond resulting generally in capital gain or loss treatment. Bonds issued prior to 1955 must be with interest coupons or in registered form in order to qualify for this treatment.[283]

Bonds Originally Issued at a Discount: Gain on the sale or retirement of bonds held by the investor for more than one year (six months and nine months for taxable years beginning before and

---

[278] Reg. 1.61-7(c)

[279] *Rickaby,* 27 T.C. 886(A) (1958); Rev. Rul. 60-284, C.B. 1960-2, 464

[280] *Jaglom,* 303 F. 2d 847 (CA-2, 1962); *Langston,* 308 F. 2d 729 (CA-5, 1962)

[281] Rev. Rul. 72-521, C.B. 1972-2, 178 (replacing I.T. 3989, C.B. 1950-1, 34). The earlier ruling, specifically dealing with dividends paid on short sales, has been cited as applicable to interest paid on borrowing of securities, although the interest was disallowed on grounds of sham. J. G. Gold, 41 T.C. 419, 426, (1963).

[282] *Hart,* 41 T.C. 131 (1963), aff'd. 338 F. 2d 410 (CA-2, 1964) (See footnote 372).

[283] Code: 1232(b)(2)

in 1977, respectively) and which were originally issued (after 1954) at a discount of more than $\frac{1}{4}$ percent a year is given special treatment.[284] That portion of the gain which represents the original discount element is treated as ordinary income, with excess gain, if any, given capital gain treatment.[285] In the case of convertible bonds, the issue price is not reduced by the value of the conversion feature in determining original issue discount.[286] Where bonds are issued with detachable warrants, however, a portion of the issue price must be allocated to the warrants, and thus original issue discount may result.[287] Allocation of each element of the investment unit is made on the basis of relative market values. A failure to exercise warrants issued as part of the investment unit will not affect the amount of original issue discount determined at the time the bonds were issued.[288] If a loss is realized on disposition of the bond, it is treated as a capital loss. For the treatment of original issue discount on obligations issued after May 27, 1969 see page 114. The original discount rule generally does not apply to tax-exempt bonds or bonds purchased at a premium. However, gain on sale of tax-exempt bonds attributable to original issue discount is treated as tax-exempt interest, while the gain attributable to market discount is taxed as capital gain.[289] Similarly, accrued interest income and original issue discount, including unearned discount, received on redemption of tax-exempt bonds prior to maturity date represent tax-exempt income, but any premium paid represents gain from exchange of the bonds.[290] Where dealers acquire a series of bonds from a governmental unit at par and sell some of the bonds to the public at a discount, the Treasury has ruled that the discount is not tax-exempt.[291]

The discount on noninterest-bearing federal or municipal obligations, which are payable within one year of the date of issue, will be considered as being received when the obligation is disposed of or redeemed.[292] The excess of proceeds over basis is taxed as ordinary income in the case of federal obligations.[293] In the case of municipal obligations, the gain attributable to original issue dis-

---

[284] Code: 1232(a)(2)
[285] Rev. Rul. 75-117, C.B. 1975-1, 273
[286] Reg. 1.1232-3(b)(2)
[287] Code: 1232(b)(2); Reg. 1.1232-3(b)(2)
[288] Rev. Rul. 72-46, C.B. 1972-1, 50
[289] Rev. Rul. 60-210, C.B. 1960-1, 38

[290] Rev. Rul. 72-587, C.B. 1972-2, 74
[291] Rev. Rul. 57-49, C.B. 1957-1, 62; Rev. Rul. 60-210, C.B. 1960-1, 38, modified by Rev. Rul. 60-376, C.B. 1960-2, 38
[292] Code: 454(b)
[293] Code: 1221(5)

count is tax exempt, while gain attributable to market discount is taxable as ordinary income.[294] For a discussion of Treasury bill futures, see page 110.

Sale and Repurchase: A common practice for owners of tax-exempt or other securities is to agree to sell the securities to a broker or bank at a fixed price and then repurchase the same amount of securities at the same price plus interest. This type of transaction was treated as a secured loan with the investor entitled to the tax-exempt interest income.[295] Any interest deduction would probably be disallowed if the loan was secured by tax-exempts. (See page 125.) It is understood that the Treasury is currently reconsidering its position. Under consideration is a new approach whereby the sale would be treated as a taxable sale unless identical securities are returned to the seller. While gain would be taxable on the sale, any loss would be disallowed under the wash sale provision. Future private rulings will not be issued on this point until the matter is resolved. Rev. Rul. 74-27 has been distinguished by the Treasury on the grounds that identical securities were returned. A change of position may open up new avenues for tax planning including artificially recognizing gain on the transaction where advisable or enabling the broker or bank to receive tax-exempt income and in exchange the investor may obtain better terms for the loan.

Holding that the transaction is taxable merely because the identical securities are not returned to the investor is inconsistent with other rules dealing with securities held by brokers on behalf of investors. In the latter situation, no taxable exchange results merely because the original certificates are not returned to the investor. In a sale and repurchase transaction, the securities are merely collateral for a loan and economic ownership does not pass. A sale does *not* take place (the terminology "sale and repurchase" is misleading). It should not matter that the same securities are not returned or whether or not tax-exempt securities are involved.

---

[294] Rev. Rul. 60-210, C.B. 1960-1, 38; Code: 1221(5)

[295] Rev. Rul. 74-27, C.B. 1974-1, 24; *First National Bank in Wichita*, 57 F. 2d 7, (CA-10, 1932), Cert. den. 287 U.S. 636; *American National Bank of Austin*, 421 F. 2d 442 (CA-5, 1970), Cert. den. 400 U.S. 819; but see *Bank of California, National Ass'n.*, 80 F. 2d 389 (CA-9, 1935), and *Citizens National Bank of Waco*, 551 F. 29 832 (Ct. Cl, 1977), to the contrary where the securities were not always repurchased.

Bonds with Coupons Detached: Gain realized on sale of bonds purchased after 1957 with coupons detached will be given ordinary income treatment to the extent of the market value of the detached coupons at the time of purchase.[296] Thus, if the bonds with coupons attached had a value of $900 but were sold for $800 without the coupons, the first $100 of gain on subsequent sale of the bonds would be ordinary income. Note that this provision does not affect the original seller of the bonds. Under the general rules he would apparently realize a capital gain or loss on sale of bonds with detached coupons and will report the interest on the detached coupons in gross income when received.

Detached bond coupons: Proceeds from the sale of detached bond coupons are taxed as ordinary income rather than capital gains since the coupons are not capital assets.[297] Once the bond coupons are sold, they lose their character as interest income and become capital assets.[298] Therefore, a purchaser of detached bond coupons will realize capital gain or loss on the sale of the unmatured coupons.[299] Any gain from the sale of matured bond coupons is taxed as ordinary income.[300]

Exchange of Bonds—Deferral of Gain or Loss

Ordinarily an exchange of bonds for other securities, stock or property is a taxable exchange.[301] Capital gain or loss results from an exchange of a note, secured by a real estate mortgage, for a corporate bond of the same par value but with a different market value. Unpaid interest on the note is not taxed to the noteholder because the value of the property received in exchange is less than the face value of the note.[302] Similarly, an exchange of New York City bonds for "Big MAC" bonds constitutes a taxable exchange since the bonds are not considered substantially identical. The difference between par value and the market value of the "Big MAC" bonds represents original issue discount and is exempt from tax on a subsequent sale or redemption.

Special rules, however, permit tax-free exchanges of bonds for other bonds, securities or stock, bonds in the same or a lesser prin-

---

[296] Code: 1232(c); Reg. 1.1232-4
[297] R. H. Shafer, 204 F. Supp. 473 (DC Ohio, 1962), aff'd per curiam 312 F. 2d 747 (CA-6, 1963)
[298] Sol. Op. 46, C.B. 3, 90, declared obsolete by Rev. Rul. 68-575, C.B. 1968-2, 603
[299] Rev. Rul. 54-251, C.B. 1954-2, 172
[300] Ibid
[301] Code: 1031(a)
[302] Rev. Rul. 73-328, C.B. 1973-2, 296

cipal amount (interest rates may vary), or stock in connection with a tax-free reorganization.[303] Conversion of bonds by their terms into stock of the debtor corporation also constitutes a tax-free exchange,[304] but not a conversion into stock of another corporation.[305] Gain on the receipt of long-term debentures in a corporate acquisition could be deferred on sales made prior to May 28, 1969 by electing the installment method for reporting gains.[306] The receipt of convertible debentures on sale of property could qualify for installment treatment since the conversion feature is considered part of the debenture and is not valued separately.[307] Where convertible debentures are received as part of the sales proceeds, the Treasury has questionably ruled that the amount of gain taxed at the time the convertible bonds are converted into stock would be based upon the value of the stock received in the exchange and would not be limited to the deferred gain. An identical position was taken that a gift of the convertible debenture would also result in tax to the grantor to the extent that the fair market value of the convertible debentures exceeded basis.[308] For sales contracted after May 27, 1969, marketable bonds or bonds payable on demand will be treated as cash in ascertaining whether the sale or exchange qualifies for the installment method under the 30 percent of sale price test.[309] Certain exchanges of U.S. obligations are also nontaxable.[310] The most common types of exchanges are the exchange of Series "E" bonds for other government obligations, resulting in deferment of accrued interest until ultimate redemption, and exchanges of one type of long-term government obligation for another pursuant to a special announcement. Published Capital Changes services generally provide the necessary information regarding exchanges of publicly held securities.

---

[303] Code: 354, 368, 371

[304] Rev. Rul. 72-265, C.B. 1972-1, 222

[305] Timken, 47 B.T.A. 494 (1942) ; Rev. Rul. 72-265, C.B. 1972-1 222; Rev. Rul. 69-135, C.B. 1969-1, 198.

[306] Code: 453

[307] Rev. Rul. 71-420, C.B. 1971-2, 220

[308] Rev. Rul. 72-264, C.B. 1972-1, 131. This harsh interpretation of Section 453(d) would result in an investor realizing a greater amount of income by electing the installment method than if he reported the full amount of gain at the time of the exchange. The intent of the installment sale provision was to alleviate a hardship caused by requiring a taxpayer to pay a tax on the entire gain realized on the sale although he received little or no cash in the year of sale, and not to impose a penalty for making the election. This point has not yet been litigated.

[309] Code: 453(b)(3) ; Rev. Rul. 75-117, C.B. 1975-1, 273

[310] Code: 1037

Certain U.S. Treasury bonds ("flower bonds") may be used after death in payment of the investor's estate tax liability at their par value. Due to the low interest yields on these bonds, they generally sell at a discount and therefore in the past a benefit could be obtained by acquiring these bonds at a discount and redeeming them at face value in payment of estate taxes. However, because the bonds are redeemable at face value, this value must be used in valuing the assets of the deceased investor's estate in computing both Federal and State estate or inheritance taxes. Inclusion at face value would therefore reduce the benefits of these flower bonds to the extent of the estate tax rates. Thus, if the effective estate tax rates were 70 percent, the benefit of utilizing flower bonds would be reduced to 30 percent of the discount. Naturally, the smaller the estate the greater the benefits from flower bonds. Previously no gain was recognized on redemption of these bonds because the basis to the estate would be their face value reported in the estate tax return. However, under the basis carryover provision applicable to decedents dying after 1979 (see page 65), the cost of the bonds, adjusted for estate taxes paid on the appreciation, generally would also be their tax basis in the hands of the estate. Consequently, a gain would be recognized under the basis carryover rules on redemption of these bonds. The gain would be long or short-term capital gain depending upon the holding period of the flower bonds (more than one year is required after 1977). Therefore, any additional capital gains tax paid on redemption could nullify the benefit from utilizing flower bonds for larger estates after 1979. Because of their low interest yields, unfavorable tax treatment, and limited issues available, it is expected that flower bonds will no longer be used as an estate planning technique after 1979, except perhaps for estates in low estate and income tax brackets.

WORTHLESS SECURITIES

If a security becomes completely worthless during the taxable year, its cost or basis is deductible as a loss from the sale or exchange of a capital asset taking place on the last day of the taxable year.[311] No deduction is allowed for partial worthlessness or decline in market value until the security is sold or exchanged in a closed

---

[311] Code: 165(g)

transaction. Mere bankruptcy is not sufficient to claim worthless stock loss if a shareholder may receive shares of the reorganized corporation.[312] Nor can a shareholder claim a theft loss where the bankruptcy was caused by the corporate management's fraudulent actions and statements if the shares were purchased in the open market.[313] However, an ordinary theft loss deduction may be claimed when the shareholders were induced to vote for merger because of misleading financial statements unless there is a reasonable prospect of recovery of the investment through the bankruptcy reorganization.[314] If a shareholder sells his stock before the recovery prospects materialize, it is understood that the Treasury will permit the unrecovered cost to be deductible as an ordinary theft loss rather than a capital loss.

Usually the deduction for a worthless stock loss is allowed in the year in which there is an identifiable event demonstrating worthlessness, such as bankruptcy of the corporation, reorganization with no provision for stockholders, cessation of business, etc. The Treasury frequently will insist that the loss was sustained in a later or earlier year than the one in which the loss was claimed on the return. A special seven-year statute of limitations for refund claims accords some additional protection to the taxpayer who reported the loss in the wrong year.[315] However, as one court has suggested, the only safe practice is to claim a loss for worthlessness in the earliest year possible and to renew the claim in subsequent years if there is any chance of its being applicable to the income for those later years.[316]

LOSS ON FAILURE TO DELIVER

A loss suffered by an investor arising from the failure of his broker to deliver stock which was fully paid was held to be an ordinary loss and not a nonbusiness bad debt (a short-term loss).[317] The investor had rescinded the purchase agreement, but because of the insolvent condition of his broker he agreed to settle for an amount less than the original purchase price. An ordinary loss was allowed because there was no sale or exchange and a

---

[312] Rev. Rul. 77-17, I.R.B. 1977-3, 6
[313] Ibid
[314] Rev. Rul. 77-18, I.R.B. 1977-3, 8
[315] Code: 6511(d)

[316] Young, 123 F. 2d 597 (CA-2, 1941)
[317] Meyer, T.C. Memo 1975-349, aff'd per curiam 1977-1 CCH Para. 9252 (CA-5, 1977)

creditor-debtor relationship did not exist between the investor and his broker. However, a loss realized on the sale of an investor's margin stock by the trustee of an insolvent brokerage firm in the course of liquidating its business resulted in a capital loss to the investor.[318]

ASSIGNMENT OF INCOME

Ordinarily, a shareholder or bond holder cannot validly assign part or all of the dividends or interest payable on the security and still retain ownership of the security.[319] The assigned income will be taxed to the assignor when paid. (See statutory exception for short-term trust on Page 148). However, an assignment of future income for consideration in a bona fide commercial transaction generally will result in ordinary income in the year of receipt.[320] A trust beneficiary who assigned his trust interest to a charity was held taxable on dividend income payable to the trust because the assignment was after the dividend declaration date.[321] In this ruling the date of declaration was the same as the record date, but the record date is usually controlling with respect to which shareholders are entitled to the dividend. On the other hand, an assignment of future dividend income to the shareholder's son for adequate consideration to enable the shareholder to utilize large interest deductions in the current year was upheld on the grounds that the transaction was not a sham.[322] The payment of adequate consideration, the dividend was from a publicly held corporation not controlled by the assignor, and the fact that the assignor was not required to perform future services in order to fulfill his obligations are important factors in determining whether the assignment will be recognized for tax purposes. This type of assignment is distinguishable from a sale of future rents, future manufacturing profits or future pipeline revenues where the purchasers had to look solely to the sellers to produce the future income.[323]

Note that a sale of a production payment, i.e., a right to a specified amount of future receipts from mineral property, by the owner of

---

[318] Rev. Rul. 74-293, C.B. 1974-1, 54

[319] Lucas v. Earl, 281 U.S. 111 (1930); Helvering v. Horst, 311 U.S. 112 (1948)

[320] P. G. Lake, Inc. 356 U.S. 260 (1958)

[321] Rev. Rul. 74-562, C.B. 1974-2, 28

[322] Stranahan Est. 472 F. 2d 867 (CA-6, 1973), rev'g. T.C. Memo 1971-250

[323] Mapco Inc., 76-2 USTC Para. 9622 (Ct. Cl. Trial Div.), adopted with modification 77-1 USTC Para 9476

the property to an investor or financial institution is treated as a loan rather than a sale of property.[324]

EXPENSES OF THE INVESTOR

In General   Ordinary and necessary expenses paid or incurred by an investor for the production or collection of income or for the management or conservation of his investments are deductible.[325]

Types of Deductible Expenses   Items of investor's expenses which have been held deductible include investment counsel fees, statistical services, safe-deposit box rental, custodian fees, legal and accounting advisory services, office expenses, and secretary's salary.[326] However, for post-1975 years an investor cannot deduct a portion of the expense of his residence used for investment activities unless he qualifies as a trader and meets other tests, including that the portion of the dwelling be used exclusively and on a regular basis for business purposes.[327]

Carfare to visit broker for consultation is deductible,[328] but not trips to a broker's office to watch the "ticker tapes." [329] Expenses incurred in searching for new investments have been disallowed.[330] Travel expenses incurred by an investor while making planned systematic investigations of publicly held corporations in which he held substantial interests were deductible because it was not a disguised personal trip.[331]

The Treasury has ruled that expenses incurred by stockholders in attending stockholders' meetings for the purposes of securing information on which to base future investment decisions are not deductible.[332] This questionable ruling is based on the theory that the expenses were not sufficiently related to the shareholder's investment activity so as to be deductible for income tax purposes. However, where the investor incurs reasonable expenses which are directly related to *present* investment interests, as, for example, the

---

[324] Code: 636
[325] Code: 212
[326] Reg. 1.212-1(g)
[327] Code: 280A as amended by 1976 TRA: 601
[328] *Henderson*, T.C. Memo. 1968-22
[329] *Walters*, T.C. Memo. 1969-5

[330] *Weinstein*, 420 F. 2d 700 (Ct. Cl. 1970)
[331] W. R. Kenney, 66 T.C. 122 (1976)
[332] Rev. Rul. 56-511, C.B. 1956-2, 170; however, see *Godson*, 5 TCM 648 (1946); *Goldner*, 27 T.C. 455 (1956)

attendance at a stockholders' meeting in which the value of the investor's stock or the amount of the dividends payable may be affected, the deduction of such expenses should be allowed.[333] Expenses incurred in stockholders' proxy fights have been held to be deductible.[334]

No deduction is allowed for expenses incurred which are allocable to tax-exempt income.[335] Custodial fees are disallowed to the extent attributed to services performed for tax-exempt securities.[336] Expenses that are not clearly allocable to either taxable or tax-exempt income are generally apportioned on the basis of the ratio of each to the total gross income.[337] Inclusion of capital gains, before deduction of capital losses, in gross income for purposes of allocating indirect expenses between taxable and non-taxable income is acceptable to the Treasury because there is no material distortion of income.[338] Similar rules apply to tax-exempts held in trust.[339]

Effect of Receipt of Tax-Exempt Income

State and local transfer taxes paid on the sale of securities are deductible against ordinary income if the taxpayer itemizes his deductions and, therefore, should not be deducted from the selling price in computing gain or loss on the sale.[340] See page 49 for an example of the tax saving which can be achieved.

Transfer Taxes

Limitations have been imposed on the deductibility of investment interest expense. Since 1969 the investment interest expense has been exposed to three separate treatments. Beginning in 1976 the amount of deductible investment interest expense is $10,000 ($5,000 for a married individual filing separately), plus net investment income (dividends, interest rents, royalties, short-term gains and gains on sale of investment property that is taxed as ordinary income, less other investment expense).[341] Any disallowed investment interest expense is carried over for an unlimited period to succeeding years subject to the interest expense limitation for that year.[342] Carryovers from pre-1976 years and

Interest

---

333 Cf. Milner Est., 1 TCM 513 (1943)
334 *Surasky*, 325 F. 2d 181 (CA-5, 1963); *Graham*, 326 F. 2d 878 (CA-4, 1964); followed by Treasury if cost of proxy fight connected with production of income, Rev. Rul. 64-236, C.B. 1964-2, 64; however, see *Dyer*, 352 F. 2d 948 (CA-8, 1965)
335 Code: 265(1)
336 *Alt*, 28 TCM 1501 (1969)
337 Rev. Rul. 63-27, C.B. 1963-1, 57
338 Rev. Rul. 73-565, C.B. 1973-2, 90
339 Rev. Rul. 61-86, C.B. 1961-1, 41
340 Code: 164(a); Rev. Rul. 65-313, C.B. 1965-2, 47
341 Code: 163(d)(1) as amended by 1976 TRA: 209(a)
342 Code: 163(d)(2) as amended by 1976 TRA: 209(a)

interest from certain pre-September 11, 1975 debts are still subject to the limitations in effect for 1975 (see below).[343] Proration of the net investment income is required if the investment interest expense is subject to both the old and the new limitations.[344] For example, if the net investment income is $50,000 and the investment interest expense is $100,000 of which $60,000 is attributable to pre-September 11, 1975 debt, $30,000 (60% of net investment income) of the net income is applied to determining the limitation for the pre-September 11, 1975 interest and the remaining $20,000 will be included in computing the post-1975 limitation. Thus, the post-1975 limitation is $30,000 ($10,000+$20,000 net investment income) resulting in an excess investment interest of $10,000 ($40,000 interest less $30,000 limitation). The 1975 limitation is $57,500 ($25,000+$30,000 net investment income+$\frac{1}{2}$ of $5,000 excess), resulting in excess interest expense of $2,500 ($60,000 interest less $57,500 limitation). The result is allowable interest expense of $87,500, a carryover of post-1975 disallowed interest expense of $10,000 and a carryover of pre-1976 disallowed interest expense of $2,500.

If in the above example there was also interest from certain pre-December 19, 1969 debt, such interest would be deductible without limitation.[345] Starting in 1976 this provision is applied on an allocation basis rather than a specific item basis.

For years beginning after 1971 and before 1976, the allowable amount of investment interest expense is $25,000 plus net investment income (including long-term capital gains), plus one-half of the investment interest expense in excess of the previously determined allowable amount.[346] Note that under the post-1975 limitations, long-term capital gains are not includible in net investment income. On the other hand, for pre-1976 years, the 50 percent long-term capital gain deduction may not be taken to the extent the investment interest expense is allocated to the long-term capital gains. Any disallowed interest will be carried over to subsequent years subject to the interest expense limitation for such year. As explained above, the carryovers retain their character as pre-1976 disallowed interest expense when carried over to post-1975 years.

---

[343] 1976 TRA: 209(b)
[344] Code: 163(d)(3)(A) as amended by 1976 TRA: 209(a)

[345] Code: 163(d)(5) as amended by 1976 TRA: 269(a)
[346] Code: 163(d)(1) before amendment by 1976 TRA

There was no limitation in effect for the years 1970 and 1971, but the excess interest expense (in excess of passive investment income, such as interest, dividends, rents, royalties and short-term gains less other investment expense) is treated as a tax preference item for purposes of the 10 percent minimum tax in effect for those years.[347]

Interest incurred for personal reasons, such as a mortgage on the family home or installment obligations to purchase appliances, are not subject to the limitations. Nor are loans incurred for business purposes subject to limitations. Indebtedness incurred to purchase a real estate syndicate interest or similar tax shelter will probably be treated by the Treasury as an investment borrowing and it will therefore limit the deduction of any interest incurred with respect to such investment, but any borrowings by the partnership itself for business purposes should not be subject to any limitations. Whether the real estate partnership is actively engaged in a trade or business will depend upon its activity. If it is in the business of renting real property, or operating a motel or hotel, then it is engaged in a trade or business. However, if it is merely holding vacant land for appreciation, it would not be considered engaged in a trade or business,[348] and, accordingly, any interest expense incurred would be subject to limitations. Property subject to a net lease will be treated as investment property rather than business property if (i) the deductions allowed under Section 162 is less than 15 percent of the rental income from the property, or (ii) the lessor is either guaranteed a specified return on his investment or is guaranteed in whole or in part against loss of income.[349] Note that the investment interest limitation is increased by any excess deductions incurred on property subject to a net lease.[350]

Interest on a margin account is deductible by a cash-basis investor in the year in which credits are made to the account sufficient to absorb the interest charge.[351] No deduction is allowed for interest paid on indebtedness incurred or continued to carry tax-exempt

---

[347] Code: 57(a)(1). Note that interest expense and other investment expenses may be treated as tax preferences to the extent certain non-business deductions exceed 60 percent of adjusted gross income. Code: 57(b) as amended by 1976 TRA: 301(c).
[348] Prop. Reg. 1.57-2(b)(2)(i)
[349] Code: 163(d)(4)
[350] Code: 163(d)(1)(B)
[351] Rev. Rul. 70-221, C.B. 1970-1, 33

bonds, interests in a unit trust or partnership, or shares in a municipal bond fund.[352] This would include a purchase of tax-exempts for cash in one brokerage account and a purchase by the same investor of taxable securities on margin in another account.[353] It is not necessary to trace the loan to the tax exempts, but merely to show a "sufficiently direct relationship."[354] Interest expense incurred on loans for business purposes, or personal purposes, such as to purchase a home, automobile or home appliances do not have a sufficiently direct relationship.[355] Note that refinancing an existing mortgage in order to purchase tax-exempts will result in a disallowance of the mortgage interest expenses.[356] Disallowance will result from borrowings to acquire non-business portfolio investments, e.g., stock and securities (other than substantial ownership interest such as 80 percent control), real estate investments, or limited partnership interests in real estate, farm or gas and oil syndications, or similar tax shelters.[357] Once a direct relationship is shown, the interest expense will be disallowed even if it exceeds the tax-exempt income.[358] Generally, where an individual's investment in tax-exempts is insubstantial (i.e., average adjusted basis of tax-exempts does not exceed 2 percent of average adjusted basis of investment portfolio) and there is no direct relationship between the borrowings and the tax-exempts, including the use of tax-exempts as collateral, there will be no disallowance.[359] Nor should there be a disallowance where the spouses file a joint return and one spouse purchases tax-exempts with his or her funds and the other spouse incurred investment interest expense.[360] Similarly, there should be no disallowance where an estate or trust owns tax-exempts, and a non-grantor beneficiary has incurred investment interest expense. Where an investor is also a partner in an investment partnership, however, his average investment in tax-exempts and total investments must be aggregated with his prorata share of the partnership's average investment in

[352] Code: 265(2) and (4) ; *Illinois Terminal Railroad Co.*, 375 F. 2d 1016 (Ct. Cl., 1967) ; *Wisconsin Cheeseman, Inc.*, 388 F. 2d 420 (CA-7, 1968)

[353] *B. H. Jacobson*, 28 T.C. 579 (1957) (Acq.) ; Bernard P. McDonough, T.C. Memo. 1977-50

[354] *Wisconsin Cheeseman*, supra; *Ball*, 54 T.C. 1200 (1970)

[355] Rev. Proc. 72-18, Section 4.02, C.B. 1972-1, 740

[356] Amedeo Louis Mariorenzi, T.C. Memo. 1973-141, aff'd. 490 F. 2d 92 (C.A. 1, 1974)

[357] Rev. Proc. 72-18, Section 4.04, C.B. 1972-1, 740

[358] J. S. Wynn, Jr., 411 F. 2d 614 (CA-3, 1969), Cert. Den. 396 U.S. 1008 (1970).

[359] Rev. Proc. 72-18, Section 3.05, C.B. 1972-1, 740

[360] Levitt, 368 F. Supp. 644 (1974), rev'd. on other grounds 75-1 USTC 9508; Bernard P. McDonough, T.C. Memo. 1977-50

tax-exempts and total assets in computing the amount of disallowance of investment interest expense for both the investor and his partnership.[361]

Interest paid on genuine indebtedness without collusion between the investor and the creditor to avoid income taxes will be allowed as a deduction.[362] There should be some economic substance to the transaction apart from income tax effect.[363] Interest deductions were denied where the court found that the transaction was not a "sham" but lacked a business purpose.[364] In addition, the Treasury had reversed its prior position and would allow a deduction for interest prepaid for only a 12 month period after the end of the taxable year, provided there was no distortion of income. Any remaining prepaid interest had to be deferred and deducted over the term of the loan.[365] Commencing in 1976 prepaid interest must be capitalized and deducted over the period of the loan as if the investor were on the accrued basis.[366] Thus, if an investor prepaid interest of $130 for one month in 1977 and the entire year of 1978, only $10 would be deductible in 1977 and the balance of $120 in 1978. The new provision will not apply to prepayments made before 1977 pursuant to a binding loan or contract in effect on September 16, 1975.[367] Presumably, the Treasury's one year prepayment rule would apply to these prepayments.

Amounts paid by investors as premiums for the use of stock borrowed to effectuate short sales of stock or to reimburse the lender of the stock for ordinary cash dividends paid on the borrowed stock are deductible as non-business expenses.[368] Although never specifically enunciated by the Treasury, the same should be applicable to interest paid on short sales of deben-

Dividends and Interest Paid on Short Sales

---

361 Bernard P. McDonough, T.C. Memo. 1977-50

362 *L. L. Stanton,* 34 T.C. 1 (1960)

363 *E. D. Goodstein,* 267 F. 2d 127 (CA-1, 1959); *Knetsch,* 364 U.S. 361 (1960); *Barnett,* 44 T.C. 261 (1965), aff'd 364 F. 2d 742 (CA-2, 1966); *Goldstein,* 364 F. 2d 734 (CA-2, 1966). This latter case denies deduction of prepaid interest on a "valid" indebtedness where there is no purpose for the transaction other than to obtain a tax deduction. See also *Gilbert,* 248 F. 2d 399, 411 (CA-2, 1957)

364 *Rothschild,* 407 F. 2d 404 (Ct. Cl., 1969)

365 Rev. Rul. 68-643, C.B. 1968-2, 76

366 Code: 461(g) as amended by 1976 TRA: 208(a)

367 1976 TRA: 208(b)(2)

368 Rev. Rul. 72-521, C.B. 1972-2, 178; Rev. Rul. 62-42, C.B. 1962-1, 133; *Dart,* 74 F. 2d 845 (CA-4, 1935); *Wiesler,* 161 F. 2d 997 (CA-6, 1947); contra, *Levis Estate,* 127 F. 2d 796 (CA-2, 1942)

tures.[369] These payments do not constitute investment interest expense but are deductible in computing net investment income. (See page 125 for limitations on investment interest expense.)

The Treasury has ruled that amounts paid with respect to stock dividends or liquidating dividends on stock borrowed incident to a short sale are capital expenditures and are not deductible.[370] However, an argument can be made for treating the payment of all short dividends, including stock and liquidating dividends, as an ordinary deduction, since they are merely contractual expenses incurred as a necessary cost of obtaining the borrowed stock.[371]

Where the sole purpose for entering into a short sale transaction is tax avoidance without any expectation of financial gain, the short dividends paid will not be allowed as a deduction on the grounds that they are not ordinary and necessary expenses paid or incurred for the production of income.[372] However, where there is a possibility of economic gain, even though the primary purpose is tax savings through the creation of capital gain and ordinary deductions, a strong argument could be made for the deductibility of the dividends paid on the short sale.

TAX-FREE EXCHANGES

Reorganizations

Recognizing that normal commercial activities would be impeded if every exchange or securities were subjected to income tax despite the lack of any substantial change in the security holder's financial position, Congress has enacted through the years many special tax provisions exempting certain transactions from tax. An exchange of common or preferred stock for stock of another

---

[369] I.T. 3989, C.B. 1950-1, 34 (replaced by Rev. Rul. 72-521, C.B. 1972-2, 178) has been cited for such proposition (although interest was disallowed on grounds of sham). J. G. Gold, 41 T.C. 419, 426 (1963). "It is, of course, true that one who borrows securities in order to make a short sale may deduct the amount of interest or dividends which he pays to the lender in order to reimburse him for the interest or dividends that the lender would have received during the period of the loan."

[370] Rev. Rul. 72-521, C.B. 1972-2, 178

[371] *Main Line Distributors, Inc.*, 321 F. 2d 562 (CA-6, 1963)—disallowed deduction on other grounds. Cf. *1955 Production Exposition Inc.*, 41 T.C. 85 (1963)

[372] *Hart*, 41 T.C. 131 (1963) aff'd 338 F. 2d 410 (CA-2, 1964); cf. *Carl Schapiro*, 40 T.C. 34 (1963), 39. In the *Hart* case, the transactions were mere "bookkeeping" entries with no borrowing of securities, no payment of margin, lack of investment interest, price adjustments to prevent economic substance and no delivery of stock to cover the sale.

corporation in a statutory merger or consolidation,[373] or the exchange of common or preferred stock for other common or preferred stock of the same corporation in a recapitalization[374] falls within this class. The receipt of preferred stock in a reorganization may be treated similar to a dividend of preferred stock and, therefore, may result in ordinary income on its sale or redemption.[375] Other exempted transactions include an exchange by a corporation of its voting stock for stock of another corporation which it controls after exchange,[376] a "triangular merger" using stock of the parent of one of the merged corporations,[377] and exchange of bonds for bonds (not in excess of the principal amount surrendered) or stock of the same corporation,[378] the conversion of convertible bonds into stock of the same corporation,[379] and, in appropriate cases, the receipt of stock upon division of a corporation.[380] Published Capital Changes services generally contain the information the investor needs to determine the proper tax treatment of exchanges of publicly-held securities.

With respect to the basis and holding period of the securities acquired in the exchange, see pages 64 and 71.

Involuntary Conversions—Governmental Orders

Special provisions deferring the recognition of gain or loss are applicable to investors who were compelled to surrender their securities or receive distributions from their corporations pursuant to order issued by the F.C.C.,[381] S.E.C.,[382] or the Board of Governors of the Federal Reserve System.[383] Prorata distributions of stocks and securities to shareholders of qualified bank holding companies required to divest their interests pursuant to the Bank Holding Company Act are also non-taxable.[384] Published Capital Changes services generally describe the proper tax treatment in these situations.

Exchange Funds

Holders of appreciated marketable securities formerly were able to diversify their holdings without recognition of gain by exchanging these securities for stock of a mutual fund which was specifically organized for this purpose. As a result of a change in the

---

[373] Code: 368(a)(1)(A)
[374] Code: 368(a)(1)(E)
[375] Code: 306(c)(1)(B)
[376] Code: 368(a)(1)(B)
[377] Code: 368(a)(2)(D),(E)
[378] Code: 354; 368

[379] Rev. Rul. 72-265, C.B. 1972-1, 222
[380] Code: 355; 368(a)(1)(D)
[381] Code: 1071
[382] Code: 1081
[383] Code: 1101
[384] Ibid

law, such exchanges made after June 30, 1967 will be treated as taxable exchanges.[355] Similar legislation was enacted to deny tax-free treatment on transfer of appreciated assets to an unincorporated investment company (partnership, trust, common trust fund), or where an undiversified investment company (more than 25 percent of its assets invested in one corporation or more than 50 percent invested in up to five corporations) enters into a reorganization with one or more investment companies.[356]

Other Types For discussion of tax-free exchanges of government bonds, see pages 9 and 120.

SALES TO RELATED PERSONS

Sales between related parties are viewed with suspicion by the Treasury and are strictly regulated by the Internal Revenue Code.[387] Gains realized in such transactions are generally recognized for tax purposes. Losses incurred will be disallowed for tax purposes if a member of the investor's family (spouse, descendant, ancestor, or sibling) buys the securities directly from the investor or buys them indirectly on an exchange on or about the same date and at approximately the same price.[388] The losses are not offset by gains realized on other sales.[389] The disallowed loss may be used by the purchaser to the extent the purchaser sells the security at a gain.[390] Whether the wash sale provisions can be avoided by having a related person reacquire the security is discussed on page 82.

Inter-family sales of securities can qualify for installment sales treatment, but both the Internal Revenue Service and the judiciary will closely scrutinize the transaction. An installment sale of securities to the seller's husband was approved by the court where the husband sold the securities after holding them for five months and used the proceeds to satisfy contractual obligations.[391] However, the Tax Court in a subsequent case upheld the Treasury's contention that the sale lacked substance because of the absence of a business or personal purpose other than tax avoidance where the wife sold

---

[385] Code: 351(a), (d)
[386] 1976 TRA: 2131. Generally effective for transfer after February 17, 1976 with respect to partnerships and corporations, and April 8, 1976 with respect to trusts and common trust funds.

[387] Code: 267
[388] *J. P. McWilliams*, 331 U.S. 694 (1946)
[389] *Reddington*, 131 F. 2d 1014 (CA-2, 1942); *Englehart*, 30 T.C. 1013 (1958)
[390] Code: 267(d)
[391] Nye v U.S., 75-1 USTC Para. 9510 (D.C.N.C., 1975)

the securities on the same day and reinvested the proceeds in mutual funds.[392] Prior to these cases, the Fifth Circuit approved an installment sale to trusts created for the benefit of the seller's children of stock of a corporation which was to be liquidated shortly.[393] This decision has been distinguished in subsequent cases and should be viewed with caution.

SMALL BUSINESS INVESTMENT COMPANY STOCK

A magic formula of capital gains and ordinary losses applies to sales of small business investment company stock.[394] Losses are fully deductible by any stockholder without limitation and, if in excess of the current year's income, may be carried back or forward as a business loss. Transactions with regard to SBIC stock do not have to be "netted" with one another.[395] Therefore, if a taxpayer had gains and losses in the same year on SBIC stock, the gains would be accorded capital gain treatment, while the losses would be deductible as ordinary losses. The Treasury has ruled that a loss sustained on the closing of a short sale of stock of a small business investment company is treated as a short-term loss and not as an ordinary loss.[396] The beneficial tax treatment will be denied unless there is strict compliance with the tax provisions.[397]

CURRENT DISTRIBUTIONS ON STOCK

Divided income is not limited to periodic distributions of cash or property. Also included in the definition are stock redemptions which have the effect of dividends;[398] certain sales or redemptions of shares of preferred stock which were received as stock dividends on common stock;[399] stock distributions received in lieu of cash dividends;[400] sale of stock to a related corporation;[401] distributions of stock in a corporation other than the distributing corporation;[402] cash or other property received in a reorganization which has the effect of a dividend[403] and, according to the Treasury, cash paid in lieu of fractional stock dividends unless

Dividend Income

---

[392] Philip W Wrenn, 67 T.C. No. 41 (1976)
[393] Rushing, 441 F. 2d 593 (CA-5, 1971)
[394] Code: 1242
[395] Rev. Rul. 65-291, C.B. 1965-2, 290
[396] Rev. Rul. 63-65, C.B. 1963-1, 142
[397] Childs, 408 F. 2d 531 (CA-3, 1969)
[398] Code: 302
[399] Code: 306. The ordinary income taint can no longer be eliminated because of the death of a shareholder after 1976. Code: 306(c)(1)(C)
[400] Code: 305
[401] Code: 304
[402] Cheley, 131 F. 2d 1018 (CA-10, 1942)
[403] Code: 356

shareholders approve sale of fractional shares on their behalf.[404] However, a distribution is a taxable dividend only to the extent it is paid out of either accumulated or current earnings and profits.[405] Distributions received from a regulated investment company can qualify as a dividend, non-qualifying dividend, capital gain dividend, a distribution of tax-exempt interest, or as a return of capital.[406] Capital gain distributions in a year the regulated investment company had capital loss carryovers are treated as regular dividends.[407] Distributions from a real estate investment trust may qualify as non-qualifying dividends, capital gain dividends or return of capital.[408]

Published Dividend Records indicate the tax status as well as the total amount of dividends paid annually by publicly-held corporations. The same information, with greater detail regarding distributions in property, is available in published Capital Changes services.

To compensate to a very limited extent for the double taxation of corporate income, the Code provides that the first $100 of dividends received from most domestic corporations in a taxable year is exempt from tax.[409] (The exemption is $200 if the spouse also has at least $100 of dividend income and a joint return is filed.) The dividend received credit provisions are no longer in effect,[410] but dividends received by investors who have attained age 65 are eligible for the credit for the elderly.[411]

Distributions in excess of the current and accumulated earnings and profits of the distributing corporation are treated as a return of capital, reducing the basis of the stock, and, after the investor has fully recovered his cost, any excess distributions are generally taxed as capital gains.[412]

Stock Dividends A distribution of stock of the issuing corporation is generally not taxed to the stockholders. Distributions will be taxed as ordinary dividends if the stockholders have an option to receive cash or

---

404 Rev. Rul. 69-15, C.B. 1969-1, 95
405 Code: 316
406 Code: 852. A foreign tax credit may be allowed the shareholder with respect to the non-qualifying dividends. Code: 853
407 Rev. Rul. 76-299, I.R.B. 1976-32, 9
408 Code: 857(b) and (c)
409 Code: 116
410 Code: 34
411 Code: 37
412 Code: 301(c)

property in place of the stock dividend; or the distribution is made in discharge of preference dividends for the current year or the preceding year.[413] With respect to stock distributions in place of cash dividends, the Tax Reform Act of 1969 has expanded these provisions to include (i) disproportionate distributions among the holders of various classes of common stock, (ii) constructive distributions where one class of common stock receives cash dividends and another class obtains an increased interest in the corporate assets and earnings and profits or an increase or decrease in the ratio in which one class of securities may be converted into another class of stock, or (iii) a disproportionate distribution of convertible preferred stock.[414] Cash received in lieu of fractional stock dividends will be treated as ordinary income.[415] However, if the investor is given an option either to buy or to sell fractions, and the fractional dividends are sold, capital gain or loss treatment will follow.[416] The issuance of cash for fractional shares for convenience of the distributing corporation will not cause the stock distributions to be taxable under the section 305 rules.[417] Distributions of stock of other corporations generally are taxable as ordinary dividends. Certain distributions of stock of other corporations may qualify as tax-free "spin-offs." [418] (For discussion of tax basis and holding period of stock received as a stock dividend, see pages 64 and 74.)

Stock Rights

The receipt of stock rights in the issuing corporation, by itself, is not a taxable event.[419] However, distributions of stock rights will be taxed as ordinary income if the stockholders have an option to receive cash or property in place of stock rights.[420]

The issuance of rights to subscribe to the issuing companies' convertible bonds is also a nontaxable distribution.[421] No income would be realized either on the acquisition or exercise of the convertible bonds.[422] The Treasury has ruled that the receipt of rights to purchase the issuing company's non-convertible bonds is

---

[413] Code: 305
[414] Code: 305(b)(2)(5) and (c). The rules are complex with various transitional dates but generally will not apply before 1991 to distributions on stock outstanding on January 10, 1969.
[415] Special Ruling, Dec. 21, 1960
[416] Rev. Rul. 69-15, C.B. 1969-1, 95
[417] Reg. 1.305-3(c)
[418] Code: 355
[419] Code: 305
[420] Code: 305(b)
[421] *Powel*, 27 BTA 55 (1932) (Acq.)
[422] G.C.M. 13275, C.B. XIII-2, 121

taxable.[423] A distribution of short-term transferable rights, convertible into two long-term warrants and a $100 debenture upon payment of $100, is not a taxable distribution.[424] The warrants are treated as stock for purposes of Section 305,[425] and the $100 is in payment for the debentures. Thus, this ruling is compatible with the prior ruling concerning rights convertible into debentures.

Sale of a nontaxable stock right results in caiptal gain or loss. In determining such gain or loss or the basis of stock acquired upon exercise of a stock right, the basis of the "old" stock is allocated to the nontaxable right based upon the fair market value of the rights received in relation to the fair market value of the stock (including the rights) at the time of distribution.[426] Reference to a published Capital Changes service will provide the necessary percentages of allocation. However, where the fair market value of the rights at the time of distribution is less than 15 percent of the value of the stock, no allocation is made, and the basis of the rights is zero, unless the investor elects to make the allocation.[427] (See page 64.)

Stock rights received in a nontaxable distribution take on the same holding period as the stock held.[428] Thus, when the rights are sold, the holding period of the stock is "tacked-on" in determining the holding period of the rights. However, securities acquired through the exercise of the rights will not take on a "tacked-on" holding period. The holding period will start on the date of exercise.[429]

Generally, no loss is recognized as a result of the failure to exercise nontaxable rights, unless the rights were acquired for a valuable consideration (e.g., acquired by purchase). No adjustment is made to the basis of the stock with respect to which the expired rights were distributed.[430]

Distributions by a corporation of rights to acquire stock of other

---

[423] G.C.M. 13414, C.B. XIII-2, 124. Note that in a private ruling concerning the issuance of A.T.&T. rights to acquire a unit consisting of warrants and debenture bonds of the issuing corporation, the issuance and exercise were held to be nontaxable. The ruling permitted the entire option price to be attributed to the purchase of the bond with the warrant receiving the same basis as the right.

[424] Rev. Rul. 72-71, C.B. 1972-1, 99
[425] Code: 305(d)
[426] Code: 307(a), Reg. 1.307-1
[427] Code: 307 (a), Reg. 1.307-2
[428] Code: 1223(5)
[429] Code: 1223(5); Reg. 1.1223-1(f); Rev. Rul. 56-572, C.B. 1956-2, 182
[430] Reg. 1.307-1; Special Ruling, Dec. 4, 1946

corporations have been held to be taxable at the time of exercise or sale and not at the time of issuance.[431] The amount that is taxable as a dividend cannot exceed the lower of the spreads between option price and fair market value of the stock purchased at the time the rights are issued and at time of exercise.[432] It would appear that the amount received upon sale of the right, in excess of the spreads, should be taxable as capital gain,[433] but the Commissioner has taken the position that such amount is taxable as ordinary income.[434] The Tax Court has rejected the Commissioner's contention that the proceeds of sales constitute ordinary income and not dividend income.[435]

Notwithstanding the above cited cases, the Treasury has ruled that under the 1954 Code the issuance of rights to acquire stock of another company is taxable as a dividend at the time of issuance.[436] It has distinguished these cases on the grounds that the method of taxing corporate distributions was comprehensively revised in the 1954 Code. Under its interpretation non-corporate shareholders realize dividend income at the time of receipt to extent of fair market value (corporate shareholders realize no income), and this amount is also the shareholder's basis in the rights. Upon exercise, no gain or loss is realized by the shareholders, and the basis of the acquired stock will be the option price plus the tax basis of the stock rights. A sale or lapse of the rights results in capital gain or loss. The distributing corporation will realize gain on the exercise of the rights to the extent the option price exceeds its tax basis. There have been no subsequent court decisions as to the validity of this ruling.

The courts are split as to whether a distribution of rights to stc of another corporation may qualify as a tax-free "spin-off" [437] resulting in no gain or loss or dividend income when the rights are exercised. Dividend income may result upon the sale of such rights.[438]

---

[431] *Palmer*, 302 U.S. 63 (1937); *Choate*, 129 F. 2d 684 (CA-2, 1942); *Baan*, 451 F. 2d 198 (CA-9, 1971)

[432] Ibid

[433] *Gibson*, 133 F. 2d 308 (CA-2, 1943)

[434] GCM 25063; C.B. 1947-1, 45 (declared obsolete by Rev. Rul. 71-498, 498, C.B. 1971-2, 434)

[435] *Tobacco Products Export Corporation*, 21 T.C. 625 (1954); *Baan*, 45 T.C. 71 (1965), rev'd on other grounds 382 F. 2d 485 (CA-9, 1967)

[436] Rev. Rul. 70-521, C.B. 1970-2, 72

[437] Code: 355; see *Gordon*, 382 F. 2d 499 (CA-2, 1967), rev'd 391 U.S. 83 (1968) and *Baan*, 382 F. 2d 485 (CA-9, 1967), aff'd 391 U.S. 83 (1968). The Supreme Court did not resolve this point.

[438] See *Baan* and *Gordon*, *supra*

LIQUIDATIONS

Upon complete liquidation of a corporation a shareholder will realize capital gain or loss depending upon the value of the liquidating distributions and the tax basis of the shareholder's stock.[439] The capital gain or loss treatment also applies to a one year liquidation although the corporation may escape tax on sales of property during the liquidation period.[440] Where the one month liquidation provision is elected, any gain realized by an individual shareholder will be taxed as dividend income to the extent of his ratable share of the corporation's earnings and profits, and any remaining gain will be taxed as capital gain to the extent the cash and marketable securities (acquired after 1953) received on liquidation exceed the ratable share of earnings and profits.[441] In the case of a partial liquidation, capital gain or loss will be realized depending upon the value of the liquidating distribution and the tax basis of the stock surrendered or deemed surrendered in the exchange.[442] While ordinarily not applicable to a publicly held corporation, capital gain treatment upon liquidation will be denied if the liquidating corporation is a "collapsible corporation." [443]

FOREIGN SECURITIES AND FOREIGN CURRENCY

Foreign Income Tax Withheld

An investor may at his option claim foreign income tax withheld on income received from a foreign investment as a deduction, or as a credit against the federal income tax.[444] The latter is normally more advantageous. In either case, the full amount of the dividend before withholding must be included in income.

Foreign Investment Companies

Long-term gain from the sale of a foreign investment company stock is treated as ordinary income to the extent of the investor's ratable share of the company's undistributed earnings and profits after 1962.[445] The gain will be treated as capital gain if the foreign investment company elects to distribute its income currently.[446]

---

[439] Code: 331(a). The installment method of reporting gain is not available.

[440] Code: 337

[441] Code: 333. This election is made only when the corporation has little or no earnings and profits and thus enables a shareholder to defer reporting gain on liquidation. He is also eligible to elect the installment method on sale of the property.

[442] Code: 331(b), 346; Rev. Rul. 57-334, C.B. 1957-2, 240.

[443] Code: 341(a)(2)

[444] Code: 164(a); 33; 901 et seq.

[445] Code: 1246. Similar rules apply to gains realized by an investor who owns at least 10 percent of a foreign corporation's stock. Code: 1248

[446] Code: 1247

Certain acquisitions before July 1, 1974 by United States citizens or residents, or their agents, of foreign securities or indebtedness were subject to an interest equalization tax of up to 22½ percent.[447] The rates were subject to modification by Presidential executive order. The tax was not imposed on foreign securities acquired by the U.S. investor from a U.S. person. This exemption was available only if the seller applied for and obtained a validation certificate from the Treasury.[448] Other exemptions from this tax include investments in certain new Canadian issues and investments in less developed country corporations. The tax could not be avoided merely by acquiring the foreign securities through a foreign broker.

Interest Equalization Tax

Investors in foreign currencies will realize capital gains or losses upon culmination of the transaction.[449] Foreign currency held for investment is considered a capital asset and generally is subject to the same tax rules as securities.[450] Losses on sales of foreign currencies are not subject to the wash sales rules (see page 78).[451] Gain on retirement of foreign debt was held to be ordinary income.[452] However, exchange of Mexican gold coins for Austrian gold coins, whose values were based on gold content and were not used as currency, qualified as a tax-free exchange under Section 1031.[453] Trading has recently commenced in foreign currency futures. The rules applicable to these transactions are identical to the general rules of commodity futures and are covered on page 105.

Foreign Currency Transactions

INSIDER'S SHORT-SWING PROFITS

An officer, director, or 10 percent or greater stockholder of a listed corporation or other corporation required to file annual reports with the SEC may be required to turn over to the corporation the gains realized on the sale of its stock if he sells and purchases (or purchases and sells) the stock of the corporation within a six-month period.[454] Ordinarily, the executive will realize a capital loss on repayment.[455] Tax Court decisions allowing an

---

[447] Code: 4911 to 4931, expired June 30, 1974
[448] TIR 918, July 22, 1967
[449] Rev. Rul. 74-7, C.B. 1974-2, 198; Rev. Rul. 75-479, C.B. 1975-2, 44
[450] Cf. *Frank C. LaGrange,* 26 T.C. 191 (1956)
[451] Rev. Rul. 74-218, C.B. 1974-1, 202
[452] Gillin, 423 F.2d 309 (Ct. Cl., 1970)
[453] Rev. Rul. 76-214, C.B. 1976-1, 218
[454] Section 16(b) of the Securities Exchange Act of 1934
[455] Rev. Rul. 61-115, C.B. 1961-1, 46

ordinary deduction where the payment was made solely to protect the executive's reputation have been reversed on appeal.[456] The problem is particularly likely to arise where the executive is in need of funds to exercise a stock option.[457] Instead of selling his stock, he should borrow the funds, with his stock as collateral, and sell the stock after the six-month period expires. A voluntary conversion of convertible bonds or preferred stock into common stock followed by a sale of the common stock within six months of the conversion date also comes within the short-swing profits provisions.[458] Advice of counsel should be obtained in all doubtful cases.

MINIMUM TAX

In addition to the regular income tax, after 1969 individual taxpayers must pay a minimum tax on their tax preference items that resulted in tax benefit. Beginning in 1976, a minimum tax of 15 percent is imposed on tax preference in excess of the higher of $10,000 ($5,000 for spouses filing separately), or one-half the regular Federal income tax.[459] Included in the list of tax preferences for post-1977 years are: [460]

1. Excess accelerated depreciation on real property;
2. Excess accelerated depreciation on leased personal property;
3. Excess amortization on pollution control facilities;
4. Excess amortization on railroad rolling stock;
5. Unrecognized gain on exercise of qualified or restricted stock options;
6. Excess of depletion deduction over adjusted cost;
7. Excess oil and gas intangible drilling expenses in excess of net oil income;
8. One-half long-term capital gains (60% for post-10/31/78 net capital gains); and
9. Itemized deductions (except medical and casualty losses) in excess of 60 percent of adjusted gross income.

---

[456] Mitchell, 428 F. 2d 259 (C.A.6. 1970), rev'g. 52 T.C. 170 (Cert. den. 401 U.S. 909, (1971); Brown, 529 F. 2d 609 (C.A. 10, 1976)

[457] Cf. *Greene v. Dietz*, 247 F. 2d 689 (1957); *Babbitt Inc. v. Lachner*, S.D. N.Y. 12/13/63

[458] *Park & Tilford, Inc. v. Schulte*, 160 F. 2d 984 (1947); *Heli-Coil Corp. v. Webster*, 222 F. Supp. 831 (1963)

[459] Code: 56 as amended by 1976 TRA: 301(a). The prior minimum tax rate was 10 percent and a $30,000 deduction was allowed ($15,000 for spouses filing separately) plus the current year's Federal income tax and unused tax carryovers from prior years.

[460] Code: 57 as amended by 1976 TRA: 301(d)

The last two preference items will no longer be subject to the minimum tax for years beginning after 1978 and instead will be included in an alternative maximum tax, which is discussed below.[460a] Capital gain on sale of a principal residence after July 26, 1978 will also no longer be a tax preference.

With the elimination of the capital gains deduction as a tax preference, the minimum tax provision will apply principally to investors who participate in tax shelters.

ALTERNATIVE MINIMUM TAX

To insure that all taxpayers with substantial income pay some taxes, a separate alternate maximum tax is imposed for taxable years beginning after 1978. This tax will be imposed only if it exceeds the regular income tax (including the 15% minimum tax). Only the foreign tax credit and certain refundable credits are offset against the alternate minimum tax. The alternate tax on the alternate minimum taxable income is as follows:

Income	Rate
0 to $20,000	Exempt
$20,000 to $60,000	10%
$60,000 to $100,000	20%
Over $100,000	25%

In computing the alternate minimum taxable income, an investor's gross income is reduced by (i) total deductions allowed for the year and (ii) accumulated trust income includible under Section 667; and is increased by (i) the net capital gains deduction (60%) and (ii) itemized deductions (except medical, casualty losses, state and local taxes and Section 691(c) deductions) in excess of 60 percent of adjusted gross income (reduced by medical, casualty losses, state and local taxes and Section 691(c) deductions).

This alternative minimum tax is expected to affect only those limited taxpayers who have paid little or no tax in prior years because of the capital gains deduction or the use of itemized deductions, such as interest expense or charitable deductions. Therefore, most investors can ignore this provision in their tax planning.

460a 1978 RA: 421

MAXIMUM TAX ON PERSONAL SERVICE INCOME

Commencing in 1972 the maximum tax rate for income from personal services is 50 percent.[461] Personal service income (formerly referred to as earned income) includes salaries, wages, professional fees, commissions and qualifying partnership income. After 1976 this list will also include deferred compensation (without the prior one year restriction), and pension income (other than lump sum distributions and penalty distributions from individual retirement accounts). The maximum rate applies to only a portion of the personal service income, in the same ratio as the taxable income bears to the adjusted gross income. Tax preferences (see section on minimum tax) will reduce the eligible personal service income dollar for dollar. Note that post-October 31, 1978 net capital gains no longer constitute a tax preference for these purposes. However, preference from tax shelters will still affect the maximum tax computations unless the regular tax on all taxable income is reduced to no more than 50 percent. Some investors may find it more advantageous to use the income averaging alternative. (See page 142.) Any excess earned income plus other income, such as investment income, will be taxed at the regular rates

INCOME AVERAGING FOR CAPITAL GAINS

Investors who have substantial net capital gains in the current taxable year may realize considerable savings in income tax by electing the income averaging provisions and thereby compute their tax as though the bunched income was earned over a five-year period. Income averaging is also available with respect to most types of ordinary income.[462] However, taxpayers using income averaging cannot use the capital gains alternative tax computation for pre-1979 years (see page 61) or the maximum tax on personal service income. (See page 141.)

"SHAM" TRANSACTIONS

An investor may make his investments in any legitimate manner in order to obtain the maximum tax savings, and he will not be

---

[461] Code: 1348. A maximum rate of 60 percent was in effect for 1971.   [462] Code: 1301-1305

punished for choosing the avenue that produces the lesser tax.[463] This rule does not give tax effect to mere paper transactions, where in lieu of actual purchases and sales, the alleged transactions are merely entries on the broker's books.[464] Nor can an investor have recognized for tax purposes a transaction he enters into solely for tax reasons (e.g., to obtain interest deductions in the current year) with no expectation of ever realizing a profit on the transaction.[465] Through proper planning, an investor can obtain maximum tax savings without resort to "sham" transactions.

PARTNERSHIPS

A partnership can take the form of a general business partnership, an investment club, a hedge fund, or a limited partnership with a general partner making the investment decisions. It is not a taxable entity,[466] but a conduit through which dividends, capital gains, tax exempt income and other items of income and deductions are passed through and allocated among the partners in accordance with the partnership agreement.[467] Capital gains of a fiscal year partnership whose year ends in 1977 will be subject to the six month holding period rule since the increased holding period provision applies to taxable years beginning in 1977.[468] The same principle applies to capital gains realized by a fiscal year partnership in 1978 (nine months) and 1979 (one year). An election may be made by all the members not to be treated as a partnership if the separate income and deduction can be adequately determined without the computation of partnership income.[469] It is important that the partnership avoid falling within the classification of an association which is taxed as a corporation.[470]

The Treasury has ruled that the investment activities of an investment club do not constitute business activities and therefore, the expenses of such partnership are deductible on a pro-rata basis as itemized deductions by each partner on his personal income tax

[463] *Gregory v. Helvering*, 293 U.S. 465 (1935) ; *Karl F. Knetsch*, 364 U.S. 361 (1960)

[464] *Eli D. Goodstein*, 267 F. 2d 127 (CA-1, 1959) ; *George C. Lynch*, 273 F. 2d 867 (CA-2, 1960)

[465] See *Kapel Goldstein*, 364 F. 2d 734 (CA-2, 1966) ; *Michael J. Ippolito*, 364 F. 2d 744 (CA-2, 1966) (cert. den.

385 U.S. 1005) ; *Rothschild*, 407 F. 2d 404 (Ct. Cl., 1969) ; Rev. Rul. 77-185, I.R.B. 1977-21, 7

[466] Code: 701

[467] Code: 702

[468] 1976 TRA: 1402; Code: 702(a) (1)

[469] Code: 761

[470] Reg. 1.761-1(a) (2) (i) ; Code 7701 (a) (3) ; Reg. 301.7701-2

return.[471] This questionable position is contrary to the general rule that partnership expenses are effectively deductible by the partners in arriving at adjusted gross income.

CORPORATIONS

A corporate investor generally is subject to the same rules as an individual with respect to tax basis, holding period for long-term capital gains, wash sales and short sales. The total amount of cash dividends are included in gross income, but dividends paid in property to U.S. corporate shareholders are included in gross income at the lesser of market value or the adjusted tax basis in the hands of the distributing corporation.[472]

In lieu of a $100 exclusion for dividends, a corporate shareholder is entitled to an 85 percent dividends received dividend.[473] Covered option writing for a corporation has a special attraction especially in high dividend paying stocks, since 85% of the dividend income received may be tax-free. In general, common and preferred stock must be held for more than fifteen days and preferred stock with dividends in arrears for more than 366 days, must be held for more than ninety days in order for the particular dividends to qualify for the 85% dividends received deduction.[474] The required holding period is suspended during the time the corporation owns a Put or sells the stock short.[475] Thus, the simultaneous purchase of a preferred stock and acquisition of a Put will prevent the commencement of the fifteen or ninety day holding period, thereby preventing the dividend received from qualifying for the 85% dividends received deduction. The required holding period is also suspended for any period in which the corporation "is under a contractual obligation to sell the stock."[476] The question is then whether the writing of a Call places the corporation under an obligation to sell the underlying stock. The obligation to sell occurs only when the "short Call" is exercised. Furthermore, the legislative history of Code Section 246(c) indicated an attempt to prevent the 85% dividends received deduction only when the corporation is also under the obligation to pay over to a third party the same dividend that it has received. This is not the case when the corporation is

---

471 Rev. Rul. 75-524, C.B. 1975-2, 342
472 Code: 301(d)(2)
473 Code: 243(a)(1)
474 Code: 246(c)(1), (2)
475 Code: 246(c)(3)
476 Ibid

short the Call. Accordingly, covered writing should not affect the 85% dividends received deduction.

Dividends received from affiliated members may qualify for an 100 percent dividends received deduction or are excluded from gross income if both corporations join in a consolidated return.[477] Thus, ordinarily, a corporation in 1979 would prefer to realize dividends rather than long-term gains because the maximum tax rate on dividends is 6.9 percent (15% of 46% corporate rate), whereas long-term capital gains are taxed at 28 percent. The Treasury has ruled that dividends received by a corporate investor, who had loaned stock to be used to close a short sale, do not qualify for the dividends paid deduction.[478] Until this position is litigated, corporations should consider whether to lend their shares to effectuate short sales. Dividends received by a corporation from a regulated investment company may qualify, in part or in whole, for the 85% dividends received deduction. This should be true even though the regulated investment company engages primarily in covered writing.[479] However, dividends received deductions are not allowed on distributions from "money market" funds whose gross income consists principally of interest income.

Net long-term capital gains received in post-1978 years can either be taxed at regular corporate tax rates [480] (17% first $25,000 of taxable income, 20% next $25,000, 30% next $25,000, 40% next $25,000 and 46% over $100,000) similar to short-term capital gains, or be taxed at a rate of 28 percent by means of the alternative tax computation.[481] The 60 percent long-term capital gain deduction is not available to corporations. Unused capital losses cannot be offset against ordinary income but can be carried back three years and carried forward for five years as short-term capital losses.[482] However, a capital loss cannot be carried back if it will create or increase a net operating loss for the taxable years to which the loss is being carried. Note that a capital loss must be

---

[477] Code: 243(a)(3); Reg. 1.1502-14(a)
[478] Rev. Rul. 60-177, C.B. 1960-1, 9
[479] The Regulated Investment Company must meet the 75% test of Section 854(b)(1)(B). The short-term gain recognized under Section 1234(b) does not constitute gross income for purposes of the 75% test. Code: 854(b)(3)(A). Note, however, that a regulated investment company will be disqualified if more than 30 percent of its gross income consists of gains on sale of securities held for less than three months (Code: 851(b)(3)).
[480] Code: 11 as amended by 1978 RA: 301
[481] Code: 1201(a) as amended by 1978 RA: 403
[482] Code: 1212(a)

carried back to a year in which the capital gains could be offset by net operating losses from other years.[483] Accordingly, a corporation with expiring net operating losses should not use a commodity Straddle; i.e. close out the profitable position in the year the net operating losses will expire and establish a short-term loss by closing out the loss position in the subsequent year, because any unused capital losses in the three subsequent years must be carried back and applied against the capital gain created in the expiring year before the net operating loss carryover can be offset against the capital gain. The commodity Straddle could be used if the economic circumstances justify the Straddle and more than three years Straddling transactions are not too cumbersome.

The minimum tax provisions also apply to all corporations, but personal holding companies and Subchapter S corporations are treated as individuals for this purpose.[484] While the list of tax preferences may differ somewhat from those applicable to individuals (see page 140), approximately 39% ($^{18}\!/_{46}$) of long-term capital gains constitute a tax preference if the alternative tax method is utilized.[485] Beginning in 1977, the minimum tax rate is 15 percent and the allowable deduction in computing the tax is the greater of $10,000 or regular Federal income tax for the current year.[486]

Interest received from tax-exempt securities is excluded from the corporation's taxable income.[487] However, it is includible in earnings and profits of a corporation and constitutes a taxable dividend when distributed to shareholders.[488] Despite this detriment, investment in tax-exempts may be advisable for corporations that may be liable for tax on unreasonable accumulation of earnings,[489] or the personal holding company tax.[490] Tax-exempt income is excluded in calculating the amounts subject to tax. Corporations investing in tax-exempts suffer the risk that some of their interest expense and investment expense allocable to the tax-exempt income will be disallowed, thereby reducing the tax benefits of this type of investment. Nevertheless, interest will not be disallowed if not directly attributable to the tax-exempts or the tax-exempts con-

483 Reg. 1.1212-1(a) (3) (iv), Example (6)
484 Code: 58(i) as amended by 1976 TRA: 301(d)
485 Code: 57(a) (9) (B)
486 Code: 56(a) and (c) as amended by 1976 TRA: 301
487 Code: 103
488 Reg. 1.312-6(b)
489 Code: 531
490 Code: 541

stitute not more than 2 percent of the average adjusted basis of the total business assets.[491]

Closely held corporations, with five or less individuals directly or indirectly owning at least 50 percent of the value of the outstanding stock and whose personal holding company income (dividends, interest, royalties, etc.) constitute at least 60 percent of its adjusted ordinary gross income, may be subject to a personal holding company tax of 70 percent on its undistributed personal holding company income. All capital gains are excluded in making the 60 percent test.[492] Net long-term gains, after adjustment for capital gains tax, are deducted in computing the personal holding company tax.[493] Personal holding company tax can be avoided by distributing all of the personal holding company income. The use of a personal holding company as a vehicle to hold the family's investments is recommended for estate planning since a large discount from the value of the underlying assets may be taken for gifts of minority interests to other family members or where the shareholder, including the original grantor, owns a minority interest at time of death.

A corporation (Subchapter S Corporation) may elect to be treated similar to a partnership, whereby the shareholders report on their tax returns their share of the undistributed ordinary income, long-term capital gains, or net operating losses.[494] This election is ineffective if its passive investment income (dividends, interest, rents, gains from sale of securities, etc.) exceeds 20% of its gross receipts.[495] Care should be taken to limit its passive income to 20 percent. Investment in tax-exempts may be ideal for this purpose.

ESTATES AND TRUSTS

Estates and trusts compute their taxable income in a manner similar to individuals and pay a tax on undistributed income using the tables of an unmarried individual.[496] The investment interest expense limitation is applicable, but trusts are not entitled to the $10,000 minimum deduction.[497] A deduction is allowed for dis-

---

[491] Rev. Proc. 72-18, C.B. 1972-1, 740
[492] Code: 543(b)
[493] Code: 545(b)
[494] Code: 1371-1375
[495] Code: 1372(e)(5)
[496] Code: 641
[497] Code: 163(d)(1)

tributions to beneficiaries, who must report the income in the year the estate's or trust's taxable year ends.[498] The character of the income will be the same as in the hands of the estate or trust.[499] Thus tax exempt income received by an estate or trust will retain its exempt status when received by the beneficiary.

Ordinarily, the estate or trust will pay a tax based on its income on any capital gains realized unless the governing instrument provides for distribution of capital gains.[500] However, a sale of appreciated property that was transferred within two years from the date of sale will be taxed to the trust at the same rates as if the transferor had sold the property and reported the gain realized on the sale, but not in excess of the appreciation at the time transferred to the trust.[501] The two year period cannot be avoided by a short-sale of the property ("short against the box").

A capital gains tax can be avoided on discretionary distribution of appreciated property to a beneficiary where there is no obligation to make the distribution either in a specific dollar amount or in other property.[502] For example, if a fiduciary has the discretionary power to accumulate or distribute the income, a distribution of appreciated stock or securities will not be taxed to the estate or trust and the beneficiary will report income based on the value of the property received, in a similar manner as a distribution in cash, and the market value will also be the beneficiary's tax basis for the property.

A tax-planning device that was not affected by the 1976 TRA is a ten-year reversionary trust.[503] Under this arrangement a high tax bracket individual places assets in a trust, with the income to be distributed to a dependent parent or other family members who pays little or no tax on the income because of the allowable deductions, exemptions, and low tax-bracket of the dependent. In the case of a minor child it is recommended that the income be accumulated in a custodian account with the grantor's spouse as the custodian. Any capital gains realized by the trust will be taxed currently to the grantor although not received until termination

---

[498] Code: 651 and 662
[499] Code: 652 and 663
[500] Code: 643(a)(3)

[501] Code: 644(a)(1) as amended by 1976 TRA: 701(c)
[502] Reg. 1.661(a)-(2)(f)
[503] Code: 673

of the trust unless the trust instrument provides that capital gains are to be distributed to a beneficiary other than the grantor or his spouse.[504] Upon termination of the trust, the trust principal, including any unrealized appreciation, reverts back to the grantor. Instead of making support payments or accumulating funds for the future needs of his children with after-tax dollars, through this arrangement the same needs are met with half the outlay due to the savings of tax. For example, if an individual in the 50 percent tax bracket makes yearly support payments of $3,000 to his dependent parents, he will have to earn $6,000 of before-tax income in order to make the payments. By distributing to a short-term trust sufficient funds to earn $3,000, the trust distributions are not taxed to the grantor and the beneficiaries escape tax by means of their exemptions and deductions. Therefore, the grantor saves $3,000 of tax annually or $30,000 over a ten-year period.

A U.S. grantor could defer tax until expiration of the trust by creating a foreign trust, preferably with a situs in a tax-haven country, invest the funds in foreign securities, and provide for income to be accumulated and paid to U.S. beneficiaries upon expiration of the trust.[505] The advantage of creating a foreign trust is that income could be earned on the funds which otherwise would have been used to pay taxes by a U.S. trust. Foreign trusts created before May 22, 1974 do not come within the new grantor trust provisions discussed below, but a U.S. beneficiary will be liable on receipt of the accumulated income for a nondeductible interest charge of 6 percent per annum for the year the distributed income was accumulated.[506] Foreign trusts created by a U.S. grantor after May 21, 1974 with at least one U.S. beneficiary will be treated as a grantor's trust for post-1975 years.[507] The grantor is treated as the owner of the property and must include the income earned by the foreign trust in his tax return in the year earned. Income from a foreign trust still will be excluded from U.S. tax if there are no U.S. beneficiaries. An excise tax of 35 percent of unrealized gain will be imposed on any appreciated property transferred by a U.S. person to a foreign trust, foreign corporation or foreign partnership unless the transferor treats the contribution as a taxable exchange.[508]

---

[504] Code: 677
[505] Code: 655(c)
[506] Code: 667(a) and 668 as amended by 1976 TRA: 1014

[507] Code: 679 as amended by 1976 TRA: 1013
[508] Code: 1491 and 1057 as amended by 1976 TRA: 1015

Qualified pension, profit sharing and stock bonus plans, and religious, educational, charitable and other tax-exempt organizations are not taxed on their investment income.[509] An exempt private foundation is subject to a two percent excise tax on its net investment income consisting of dividends, interest, rents, royalties and net capital gains less applicable investment expense.[510] Note that capital losses are deductible only against capital gains and any excess capital losses cannot be carried to another year. Tax-exempt income is also exempt from the two percent excise tax. Notwithstanding their tax-exempt status, any unrelated business income is subject to a regular corporate or unincorporated tax depending upon whether the exempt organization is a corporate or unincorporated charity.[511] Investment income normally is not considered unrelated business income unless derived from debt-financed property.[512] Thus, if securities are purchased on margin, the income from the securities is taxed to the extent of the percentage of the property that is debt financed, less a deduction for a similar percentage of related investment expense. Income from lapse of options regularly written by a tax-exempt organization was held by the Treasury to constitute unrelated business income,[513] but this has been rectified by recent legislation.[514] Organizations which were hesitant to write "covered" Calls (Calls in which they own the underlying stock) are now free to utilize Calls as an investment technique to maximize income on their investments. However, income on lapse of options now constitutes short-term gains and is subject to the two percent excise tax when earned by private foundations.[515]

NON-RESIDENT ALIENS

A non-resident alien investor may be subject to U.S. tax only on certain types of income from U.S. sources. The ensuing general discussion may be superseded by a treaty between the United States and the investor's country.

---

[509] Code: 501
[510] Code: 4940
[511] Code: 511
[512] Code: 512(b)(1) and (4), and 514
[513] Rev. Rul. 66-47, C.B. 1966-1, 149. Many authorities have questioned the accuracy of this ruling, feeling its conclusion is erroneous.
[514] Code: 512(b)(5)
[515] Code: 1234(b) as amended by 1976 TRA: 2136a

In general, a 30 percent tax will be withheld on fixed income received from U.S. sources, including dividends, rental income and interest.[516] Original issue discount on bonds is generally taxed when the bonds are sold or redeemed, but original issue discount is taxed currently on bonds issued after March 31, 1972 with a maturity of more than six months.[517] Interest income from deposits with banks[518] or from corporations who derive less than 20 percent of its income from U.S. sources[519] are not taxable. Generally the 30% tax is computed without deductions, such as interest on margin account, or personal exemptions.

Capital gains are not taxed unless the foreign investor is personally present in the United States for at least 183 days or the gain is in connection with a trade or business carried on in the United States.[520] Merely buying or selling securities or commodities through a broker or agent in the United States is not considered doing business in the United States. The tax treatment of income derived from writing options was not clear prior to TRA 1976. Options written after September 1, 1976 will be accorded short-term gain or loss treatment upon expiration or upon closing of the transaction, and accordingly, will be generally exempt from U.S. taxation. If the capital gain is taxable, the 30 percent tax is imposed on the entire net capital gain, after taking into account any capital losses realized in the taxable year but without any 60 percent capital gain deduction.[521] A foreign investor who is present in the United States for only a short period of time can escape U.S. tax by selling on the installment basis and receiving the income after he has left the United States.[522] If an investor owns real property in the United States, he may be able to reduce his U.S. tax by electing to treat the real property income as being connected with a United States business.[523]

A 30 percent tax will also be imposed on fixed income from U.S. sources received by a foreign corporation not connected with a United States business.[524] The rules are similar to those discussed above for non-resident alien investors.

---

[516] Code: 871 and 1441
[517] Code: 871(a)(1)(C)
[518] Code: 861(c)
[519] Code: 861(a)(1)(B)
[520] Code: 871(a)(2)

[521] Reg. 1.871-7(c)(3)
[522] Reg. 1.871-7(d)(2)(iv)
[523] Code: 871(d)
[524] Code: 881

The types of tax shelters are varied. Included among the principal tax shelters are real estate, including commercial, residential and subsidized housing, oil and gas, coal royalties, cattle feeder and breeder programs and other agricultural products, motion picture film, and leased personal property. Some of these shelters, such as leased personal property, movie ventures, and coal royalties, have been diminished as viable tax shelters for individual investors because of prior changes in the tax law or because of a toughened Treasury tax posture. Recent case law has also denied tax deductions where an unreasonable price for a motel was agreed upon by the parties, where oil drilling actually occurred in the subsequent year despite agreement to commence drilling in the current year, and where payment for prepaid feed represented a deposit rather than a binding payment. Aside from the Treasury's intensified efforts to uncover abusive tax shelters and take appropriate action, restrictive provisions have been incorporated in the 1976 TRA which have diminished the attractiveness of most tax shelters.

The diminished importance of tax shelters as an investment vehicle as a result of the 1976 TRA will cause many investors to turn to tax-exempt securities and to taxable bonds and stocks as alternative investments. Any investment, including tax-shelters, should be judged on their risk-reward ratios. In the past many tax shelters were poor investments but could still result in a substantial after tax rate of return on investment because of favorable tax treatment. This included leverage, whereby an investor could get deductions of $3 to $4 for every dollar invested because of non-recourse loans; substantial deductions in the first years through prepaid interest expense, prepaid feed, or construction period expenses; deferral of tax until the shelter is sold or a complete escape of tax if the investor were to die holding the tax shelter; and for many tax shelters long-term capital gain on ultimate disposition.

Below is a discussion of some of the restrictive provisions incorporated in the 1976 TRA and 1978 RA and their effect on specific tax shelters.

1. *"At risk"* capital: Increased leverage can no longer be obtained through non-recourse financing whereby the debtor is not per-

sonally liable.[525] The effect of this provision is to limit the total amount of allowable deductions to actual cash or property contributions and recourse financing. However, non-recourse financing will result in a higher tax basis, resulting in greater depreciation deductions in the early years and, more importantly, in larger investment credits. Because of the increased investment credit rates, qualifying property such as breeding cattle, motion picture film and commercial real estate will still benefit greatly from the use of non-recourse financing. All tax shelters, other than real estate, will be affected by the "at risk" provision.

2. *Upfront deductions:* Prior to the 1976 TRA, the Treasury permitted a deduction for one year's prepaid interest expense where there had been no distortion of income. Cash basis taxpayers are in effect now placed on an accrual basis and can only deduct prepaid interest ratably over the duration of the loan.[526] (See page 125). This will affect most tax shelters involving financing. In the same vein, interest and taxes incurred during the real estate construction period will now have to be capitalized under transitional rules.[527] The cost of producing motion picture films cannot be deducted when incurred, but are deferred until income is earned.[528] Farming syndicates can deduct expenses for feed, fertilizer, seed and other farm supplies only when consumed.[529] In addition, the cost of planting, cultivating, maintaining and developing a grove, orchard or vineyard must be capitalized where incurred prior to the productive stage.[530]

3. *Tax Preferences:* In the past, the tax preference items created by the tax shelters were not considered important because of the exemptions and deductions allowed not only in computing the minimum tax on tax preference, but more importantly, the effect on maximum tax on personal service income. (See pages 140 and 141 respectively). As a result of the new toughened provisions, the benefits of tax shelters can be greatly reduced for investors with large personal service income, such as doctors and executives. While the effect on maximum tax on personal service income can

---

[525] Code: 465(a) as amended by 1976 TRA: 204(a)

[526] Code: 461(g) as amended by 1976 TRA: 208(a)

[527] Code: 189 as amended by 1976 TRA: 201

[528] Code: 280 as amended by 1976 TRA: 210

[529] Code: 464(a) as amended by 1976 TRA: 207(a)

[530] Code: 278(b) as amended by 1976 TRA: 207(b)

be reduced by bringing taxable income down to a fifty percent rate, this will generally create a larger minimum tax liability. Future shelters will have to depend less on accelerated depreciation or intangible drilling expenses, and instead, emphasize better investment opportunities.

4. *Capital gains on disposition:* The maximum capital gains rate of 28 percent for post-1978 transactions increases the tax benefits of certain tax shelters and must be contrasted with other shelters that generate ordinary income on disposition subject to tax rates up to 70 percent. Investors should bear in mind that the deductions created by the tax shelter may be offset against personal service income subject to a maximum tax rate of 50 percent and can be recaptured at 70 percent tax rates. Gain on sale of residential property, other than certain subsidized housing, will be taxed as ordinary income to the extent of accelerated depreciation.[531] This ordinary income treatment previously applied to sale of commercial real estate, leased personal property, motion picture film and breeding cattle. A gain on sale of oil and gas property will also be taxed as ordinary income to the extent of excess intangible drilling costs.[532] In lieu of a sale, many investors have made charitable contributions of the oil and gas property. A charitable contribution deduction will not be allowed to the extent ordinary income would have resulted from a sale of the property.[533]

5. *Increased basis at death:* Due to the inability of disposing of a tax shelter during lifetime without incurring substantial tax liability, many investors had retained their tax shelters until death. At death, the deceased investor's estate or beneficiary would obtain a new tax basis for the property equal to its market value and thereby escape tax for the excess deductions previously allowed. With the three-year deferral of the basis carryover rules, a deceased investor's beneficiary will, for the time being, escape exposure to the potential tax liability that existed prior to death.[534] (See page 65.)

---

[531] Code: 1250(a) as amended by 1976 TRA: 202(a)
[532] Code: 1254(a)(1)(A) as amended by 1976 TRA: 205(a)
[533] Code: 170(e)
[534] Code: 1023 as amended by 1978 RA: 515

DEFERRED ANNUITIES

A variation of the variable annuity policy has recently received a good deal of publicity. The main selling points of these deferred annuities appear to be high guaranteed interest rates in the first years of the policy, deferral of income taxes on the income earned by the investments, and flexibility in receiving the deferred income and the principal contributed by the investor. The terms of the policies will vary among the different insurance companies.

One type of annuity is the savings annuity whereby an investor will contribute $30,000 or more in savings bank certificates, or certificates of deposit. The insurance company takes title to these certificates and the income is not taxed to the investor until he receives his annuity payments. Because the certificates do not mature for a period of time, the investor has less flexibility in making withdrawals.

Investment annuities, on the other hand, give more flexibility to the investors. Funds are contributed to the insurance company in the form of cash or securities. These annuities also provide for high guaranteed interest in the earlier years and either a lower interest rate thereafter or an interest rate dependent on the yield from investments in the investor's custodian account. An initial contribution of securities by the investor will result in gain or loss to the investor. Any gains realized after the insurance company takes title are taxed to the insurance company, but the costs are passed on to the investor by a charge to his custodian account. For this reason investment of long-term high yield bonds are better than low yield stock. The income earned on the investments is passed through to the investor as a tax-free return of investment on the theory that the annuity has not started, but this results in larger income when the investor starts receiving annuity payments. For these services an investor may be charged an original sales charge plus annual handling charges varying from 0.5 percent to 2 percent. Penalties may also be charged for premature distributions.

Inherent in the investment annuity policies and other deferred annuities is the requirement that the investor must make the investment decision or must hire investment counselors to make them. Any additional costs for investment advisory services are borne by the investor. Originally, the Treasury approved these investment annuities, but it has recently announced that the investor would be treated as the owner of the assets held in the custodian account if he had full control over future investments.[535] In this event, the investor would be taxed on the income generated by the investments as if he retained ownership.

The announcement by the Treasury with respect to investment control casts clouds over subsequent annuity policies issued with this provision. In other respects this type of annuities offers deferral of income till later years when the investor may be in a lower tax bracket and, in the meantime, the investor receives additional income from funds that otherwise would have been used to pay the income taxes imposed on the investment income. Any distributions prior to the annuity date, i.e., the date annuity payments commence, are treated as return of principal and, in effect, the tax deferral increases the income yield of the investments less the additional costs incurred ir entering into the deferred annuity arrangement. As stated previously, annuity payments made after the annuity date are taxed under the normal annuity rules,[536] and the percentage of the annuity payments that will be subject to tax will increase if prior principal payments were made. A lump sum payment to the investor's beneficiary upon the investor's death before the annuity date would be tax-free, similar to a payment of life insurance.[537] However, the insurance proceeds would be subject to estate taxes.[538] Before investing in these deferred annuities, an investor must compare the economic and tax results with other types of investments, including tax-exempt bonds.

---

[535] I.R. 1774, 3/9/77
[536] Code: 72
[537] Code: 101(a)
[538] Code: 2042

APPENDICES—INDEX OF CITATIONS

MISCELLANEOUS

INDEX

(All references are to pages)